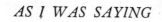

AS I WAS SAYING

AS I WAS SAYING

by

G. K. CHESTERTON

DODD, MEAD & COMPANY
NEW YORK   MCMXXXVI

≈≈≈≈≈≈≈≈≈≈≈≈≈≈≈≈≈≈

Contents

{ v }

CONTENTS

AS I WAS SAYING

OVER and above the horrible rubbish-heap of the books I have written, now filling the pulping-machines or waste-paper baskets of the world, there are a vast number of books that I have never written, because a providential diversion interposed to protect the crowd of my fellow-creatures who could endure no more. Among these, I remember, there was one particularly outrageous narrative, something between a pantomime and a parable on a variation of what the new psychologists would call a wish-fulfilment. Like most of the notions of the new psychologists, it is a notion familiar to the most far-off and antiquated fabulists. It is found in every book of folk-lore under the title of "The Three Wishes"; especially that excellent essay on the Vanity of Human Wishes, in which a man had to waste the brief omnipotence of a god in establishing right relations with a black pudding. But in my story, the black pudding was not so black or so indigestible as that producing the nightmares of Freud. Mine, like his, was such stuff as dreams are made of; but mine was only stuff and nonsense and not that perilous stuff that weighs upon the heart. So far as I remember it, it was an exceed-

ingly mad sort of story; but *that* would not have
saved it from the serious libraries of modern mental
science.

It was something about some people who had
reached so sensitized and transparent a state of imagination that when they mentioned anything it
materialized before their eyes; and this applied even
to metaphors or figures of speech which they had
not consciously conceived as material. Thus, if
two lovers were talking and taking tea in a rose-
covered cottage in a quiet English village, and one
of them happened to say, "Of course, it may be
rather a white elephant," a huge and hulking white
elephant immediately strode up the street, trampled
down the roses, and put his head in at the rose-
wreathed window. Or if the genial old squire, walking under the quiet elms of his ancestral park,
crumpled up a newspaper containing a political scandal, and said impatiently, "The man's got hold of
a mare's-nest," he would instantly behold, high
above him in the tossing top of the elm tree, the
familiar form of Black Bess out of the stables, kicking and plunging in a well-meant effort to lay eggs.
The most harmless comic man would be unable to
say "Strike me sky-blue scarlet," without a complex change in his complexion, or even to say "Till
all is blue," without transforming the whole landscape to a monochrome tint, with blue cows or blue
babies disporting themselves under a blue moon.

The effect of this, I conceive, would be to introduce a certain austerity and restraint into human speech. A plain and unadorned style would prevail in literary circles. Fastidious writers would be even more in terror of introducing a mixed metaphor; for a mixed metaphor walking down the street would be even more terrifying than such hybrids as a centaur or a griffin. But he would observe considerable economy even in making metaphors, let alone mixing them. For him, as for Mrs. Malaprop, an allegory would be as devouring as an alligator. It is a very old moral that when we get what we want we sometimes find that we do not want it; but it would be an alarming addition to the prospect if we always got anything, not only when we wanted it, but whenever we mentioned it. And the vague idea at the back of my undeveloped vision was to describe a sort of dizzy whirlwind of wish-fulfilments and dreams come true; and to suggest how intolerable such imaginative omnipotence would really be. It would be like walking upon ever-sinking and shifting shingle; on ground in which we could get no purchase for our movements or activities. A world in which the whole solidity of things had gone soft would be the essential environment of softening of the brain. We should end by shrieking aloud for the resistance of reality; ready to give up all our paradise of magic powers for the pleasure of planting our foot on a sharp nail or barking our shins upon a box. Something very like that nightmare of luxury and liberty may be felt in much of the more irresponsible or lawless literature of our own time, in which a man is driven to deny everything because he has been denied nothing; and discovers in an omnipotence to which he has no claim, an impotence for which he has no cure.

It may seem rather far-fetched to connect the nonsense about the physical metaphors with the notion about the philosophical despair. Figures of speech are risky; for in art, as in arithmetic, many have no head for figures. I will meekly claim more suitability in my symbols than there is in some of those wonderful modern analyses of the meaning of dreams; in which digging up a cabbage and putting it in a hat-box is the spontaneous spiritual expression of a desire to murder your father; or watching a green cat climb a yellow lamp-post the clearest possible way of conveying that you want to bolt with the barmaid. And metaphor does really play a special part in the sort of mad metaphysics that I have in mind. Those who suffer this particular sort of modern softening of the brain have a great tendency to preserve the metaphor long after they have lost the meaning. The figures of speech are like fossil figures of archaic fowls or fishes, made of some stonier deposit and set in the heart of more sandy or crumbling cliffs. The abstract parts of the mind, which should be the strongest, become the weakest; and the mere figures of the fancy, which should be the lightest, become the most heavy and the most hard.

Many must have noticed this in a newspaper report, and still more in a newspaper criticism. Images

that are used as illustrations are repeated without any
reference to anything that they illustrate. If the incident of the Rich Young Man in the Gospels had been
reported by a local newspaper, we should only be told
that the Teacher had called him a camel, and invited
him to jump through a needle. We should know nothing of the point of the needle—or the story. If the
Death of Socrates were condensed into a journalistic
paragraph, there would be no room for the remarks
on immortality, and not much even for the cup of
hemlock; but only a special mention of a request to
somebody to buy a cock—perhaps turned by the report into a cocktail. This often makes the art of illus-
trative argument a somewhat delicate and even dangerous occupation. When we know that people will
remember the metaphor, even when they cannot realize the meaning, it is a little perilous to choose metaphors with mere levity, even if they are quite consist-
ent with more logic. Suppose I say in some political
case that England had better go the whole hog, as did,
indeed, some of those followers of Tariff Reform who
were called Whole-Hoggers. I shall have to be very
careful to explain, somehow, that I am not really iden-
tifying the English with hogs, but that it is only
some bright facets of the hog that I compare with my
beloved country, and that the quality in question is
only a special and spiritual sort of hoggishness. Otherwise the audience, remembering everything I said
about the pig, and forgetting everything I said about
the point, will go away under the impression that I

addressed them all as swine. They will attribute to me certain familiar and even old-fashioned depreciations of the English; as that England is stupid, or England is stubborn; in short, that England is, in the apt and appropriate phrase, pig-headed. There will go along with this other notions, equally true and trustworthy; as that England has four trotters and a snout, not to mention a little curly tail behind. But, in fact, I may, in a pure spirit of lyric praise, compare my country to a pig, so long as I explain it is in the noble and exalted aspects of a pig; as that he gives us the glorious gift of bacon, or that he is said to be highly delicate and chivalrous in his relations to his lady-love; or that, being rejected by Turks and Jews, he has almost become a sacred emblem of Christendom. Otherwise, if you talk about hogs, even Hampshire hogs, you will sound like a traitor to Hampshire.

You think the mere mention of hogs could raise no such storm. I mention that the mere mention of dogs really did. I once remarked that a new religion sometimes dies before the old one; and used Goldsmith's phrase for the unexpected: "The dog it was that died." A publicist denounced me in public for calling all my religious opponents dogs! It marks the folly of fixing on figures of speech. For had he followed the meaning, and not the metaphor, he might have made a real repartee, by retorting that it was the man who survived who was mad.

WHY is it that those who admire foreign nations always ask us to admire them for the nastiest things about them? Those who abuse foreign nations are mostly mere fools, as distinct from those who abuse the abuses of foreign nations. That is quite allowable; but it is well to balance it by occasionally abusing the abuses of our own nation. In my own jog-trot journalistic exist-ence, I have generally tried to keep this balance, and to distribute abuse and vituperation in such elegant and well-chosen proportions, that nobody can be of-fended or feel that he has been left out of the fun. Those who abuse abuses are right; and even those who stare at strange uses are not very wrong. The rude forefathers of the hamlet do not always mean to be rude. Unfamiliarity breeds contempt. But not the most contemptible sort of contempt. I mean the man who laughs at a *gendarme,* when he has never in his life ventured to laugh at the much more pantomimic cos-tume of a policeman. These people, in a sense, abuse foreign nations; but it is their great glory that they admit that they laugh at them because they do not understand them, and not because they pretend that they do. But neither of these two types, the reformer who rebukes on principle or the rustic who laughs out of mere surprise, throws any light on the problem of the third kind of critic, who concerns me just now. Why, I repeat, do those who urge us to love our enemies, or merely like our neighbours, seem to have no notion of what it is that men really love or like? Why do they always point out as supreme merits the things that most normal men, if they do not actually hate, tend more or less to dislike?

We all know that one of the real Opportunities of Travel is the chance of escaping the guide and being able to contradict the guide-book. And this really is a benefit that can only be obtained by travel. If you merely stay at home, you will probably read books, and books with all the prejudices of guide-books; if not, you will read newspapers, often containing pronouncements upon Europe or America far below the mental level of any tout who tries to get a tip by showing you round an Italian ruin. In short, we all know that the real pleasures of the tripper are those that are not supposed to be part of the trip; the small, touching, humanizing sights that really do tell us that all human beings are parts of one humanity; such as the domestic scene I beheld in the most Moslem part of Palestine, the episode of a Moslem woman shouting and yelling abuse of her husband across the breadth of a small lake, while the husband stood helpless and evidently unable to think of any repartee. This made me feel, with a warm touch of sentiment, that home is home everywhere, and is not so very much altered even where a home may be a harem. Now, you cannot arrange a tour with a view to little things like that. I could no more have planned that this particular woman should boil over at this particular moment than I could pay a few *lire* to obtain an eruption of Vesuvius. But it was immeasurably more forcible and impressive than Vesuvius. For it is the little things and not the large things that touch this tricky international nerve which reminds us that we are all made on the same anatomical plan and that the Image of God is everywhere. What I complain of in the internationalist interpreters is that they seem to have no notion of what these small and attractive things are. Bring me the ordinary international pamphlet on the claims of Ruthenia, with maps and statistics and all the rest, and I shall probably end the perusal by hating the poor Ruthenians, whom I never saw and hardly ever heard of, simply because the international reconcilers do not understand why men hate or love.

I will take the hardest cases of the two nations with which, in a political sense, I am perhaps least in sympathy: Germany and Japan. The Germany praised by the Pro-Germans is much nastier than the Germany abused by the Anti-Germans. The former generally contrive to convey the impression of a human hive, of all horrible things, which very soon and very naturally becomes an inhuman hive. They give me stiff and bristling statistics about exports and imports, manufacture and machinery, strictly enforced regulations, very advanced scientific legislation, and everything else that stinks to heaven. They suggest that the German is alone industrious; by which they mean industrial. As a matter of fact, that industrial type is not generally any more industrious, if so much, as what we used to call the idle and lounging peasant of the South, who works hours before any of us dream of waking up, and sometimes hours after we go to bed; but rests in the heat of the middle of the day, not being a born fool. But, anyhow, in so far as it is true that the Germans are very industrious, did you ever hear of anybody loving anybody merely because he was industrious?

In short, it is thought an insult to call Germans sausages; but it is a compliment to call them sausage-machines. But many people like sausages, and nobody particularly likes sausage-machines. A British statesman, in the very middle of the war, solemnly told us that there are two Germanies: the bad Germany of despotism, militarism, and armed aristocracy; and the good Germany of science and commerce and chemicals used for various purposes. I remember thinking at the time, and even saying at the time, that I had much more sympathy with a soldier dying for the Kaiser than with an expert working for the Krupps. Again, one does not love experts; especially experts in poison-gas. One may fear them, and, in consequence, one may fight them. But international idealists are even now talking of Germany as the land of science and industry and technical improvement.

Now Germany is not as bad as all that. It has temptations of barbarism, and especially of mythology, but it has touches of the better mythology which is not a myth. My examples of small things would doubtless sound very small indeed. Summoned before the International Peace Conference, I should cause general disappointment if I said: "The Germans have produced one particular kind of Christmas Card which is unlike anything in the world. It really mingles the natural mystery of the forests with the preternatural mystery of the Christmas tree, and truly sets the Star of Bethlehem in a northern sky. To look at the best of these little pictures is to feel at once like a man who has received a sacrament and a child who has heard the whole of a fairy-tale. And when I look at those queer little coloured pictures, full of a sort of holy goblins, I *know* there is something in Germany that can be loved, and that perhaps is not yet lost."

I have no space to say much about the parallel of Japan, but the moral, it may be noted, is the same. Publicists have sometimes praised Japan for possessing all the qualities of Prussia, as if Prussianism were a term of praise. But I once crossed the Atlantic and watched a little Japanese playing with his little goblins of children, and I have never been quite so Anti-Japanese since.

My phrase that the Germans have a weakness for

Mythology, has been queried; but I do not use it as a mere term of abuse; for, indeed, I think I have a weakness for Mythology myself. Only I try not to regard my weakness as my strength. I could never read some huge, primitive myth about how the world was made out of a dead giant, the sky being his skull, or the sun and moon his eyes, or the sea his green blood, without wishing for one wild moment that I were the infant Hottentot or Eskimo who heard some such story from his grandmother and stood drinking it all in as innocently as I should like to do. I can never read of one of those baffling and fascinating totem-heroes who seems at once to be a man and a bald-headed eagle, or what not; and how he stole fire from the sun for the use of men, or cracked the sky to let in the upper sea, which is the rain, without wishing faintly that I were in the first morning of the world, when such things could be believed. Perhaps the Germans are still in the morning of the world. Perhaps there is that streak of truth in all their talk about their race as one descended from gods and heroes. I am well aware, however, that they have another side, which may seem paradoxically opposite; a literal and laborious side which deals with details very much in detail. And, lest some German professor should take my mythological weakness too seriously, I hasten to explain that there are no such myths as the two I have mentioned, though there are myths very similar. I made them up out of my own head. But the curious thing is that, in certain other departments, this is exactly what the Germans do.

There are certain primitive elements in the German people which are in truth faintly suggested in the very fact that they call the people a folk. To do it justice, it is a folk that is still producing folk-lore. A very agreeable product; but it must be admitted that, as in the case of the bald-headed eagle who cracked the sky, folk-lore is not always identical with fact. There are other elements that have this rather indescribable quality. We see it, for instance, in the particular *kind* of unity which the Germans exhibit from time to time. It is not, despite all their discipline, merely a disciplined unity. It is a gregarious unity. Civilization, like religion, is a thing many people are explaining, in the hope of explaining away. These connect the Commonwealth with the Herd Instinct. But I think Germany is the only nation in which it is a Herd Instinct. In a word, there is something about them that is prehistoric. Even their learned professors, in a very special sense, are often prehistoric. I mean that, learned as they are, they seem never to have heard of history.

But I repeat that this quality is not in itself odious, but sometimes almost lovable. On the whole, Mythology is a much better thing than Propaganda. Mythology is simply believing whatever you can imagine. Propaganda is, more often, believing that other people will believe whatever you can invent. There is something more than a mere manufacture of lies about the unexhausted Teuton power in the production of myths. That is why I try to be polite to the German professor, and call him prehistoric, when ruder spirits might be content to call him unhistorical. But I take it as certain that the *spirit* in the German way of telling the German story is entirely unhistorical. With all their external parade of science, their motive is not scientific. Their motive is that of a tribal tradition magnifying and exaggerating the heroes and victories of the tribe. Nobody denies that they have had heroes and victories; but the way of dealing with them is utterly out of proportion. It is quite natural that they should tell us how the spirited skirmish of Arminius cut off a few legions of Augustus. But to hear some of them telling it, one would think that Arminius had defeated the whole Roman Army and even menaced the whole Roman Empire. I doubt whether there was ever any moment in history when it could truly be said that the Teutons had conquered the Roman Empire. But it is idle to speculate about events of those remote times, when the whole point of the position is that the same thing is going on in our own time.

The extraordinary thing about Germany is that it can still produce modern myths like the ancient myths. There is something almost innocent in their spontaneity, and especially in their suddenness. They created out of nothing the story that all Teutonic barbarians, unlike all Celtic or Slavonic barbarians, were, for some mysterious reason, a race of golden-haired gods. They have created stories quite as stupendous within the last year or two. And, above all, they have credited what they created. The Teuton doubles the part of the creative poet and the credulous listener. He tells himself tales and believes them. He lives in a different world from ours; perhaps at once an older and a younger one. He explains to us, to some extent, how it was that primitive men could worship images that were obviously only imaginations. It does not matter, for the purposes of this argument, whether we think such a world of imagination lower or higher than reality. We have already heard the saying of a great German who must have really understood the Germans: "In the beginning God gave to the French the land and to the English the sea and to the Germans the clouds."

Thus there is a New Myth spread quite recently and rapidly over all Germany, almost in a few months. The New Myth is that Germany was never defeated in the Great War. You could not have a more astounding and catastrophic collision than that, between mythology and history. But the point is that the mythology is actually more modern than the history. All Germans apparently find it easy to believe it; though I can imagine few things more difficult to believe than a statement like that: that a great and somewhat arrogant Empire consented to sink the whole of its fleet and give up all its colonies, as well as nearly all its conquests in foreign countries, when it had not really been defeated. But this cloud, as it lies on the mind of a whole people, now looks as solid as a mountain. It may remain as a legend quite as fixed as that which makes Arminius rather more important than Augustus. The other part of the New Myth is that the complete surrender of all the German armies was somehow or other brought about by the Jews. I have never underrated the real problem of the international position of the Jews; but I should say that this was just about the sort of thing that the Jews alone could not possibly do. Judas could betray the Redeemer of the world; but he could hardly bribe Cæsar to surrender the Empire of the world to the Parthians.

But the point is not that you and I could never believe it in a thousand years. The point is that the Germans themselves did not believe it until within about two years. There is no evidence that the average German, for the first five or six years after his defeat, had even the faintest doubt that he had been defeated. He might think he was unjustly defeated, or unjustly treated after defeat; and he would have a right to his opinion, though there are others whose opinion I think more sound. But most of such men would have thought it sheer madness to deny the very calamity from which they suffered. These people are not the only people among whom a theorist may throw out a theory that might well appear mad. But they are the only people among whom that theory can be instantly and universally believed. To make up history after it has happened, and to make it up all different, may seem to some to have something even wildly poetical and attractive about it. But in practical politics these immense international illusions are very dangerous; and the clouds in which these people live have broken before now about us, not only in rain, but in lightning and falling fire.

WELL aware of how offensive I make myself, and with
what loathing I may well be regarded, in this sentimental age which pretends to be cynical, and in this
poetical nation which pretends to be practical, I shall
nevertheless continue to practise in public a very repulsive trick or habit—the habit of drawing distinctions; or distinguishing between things that are quite
different, even when they are assumed to be the same.
I cannot be content with being a Unionist or a Univer-
salist or a Unitarian. I have again and again blas-
phemed against and denied the perfect Oneness of
chalk and cheese; and drawn fanciful distinctions, orni-
thological or technological, between hawks and hand-
saws. For in truth I believe that the only way to say
anything definite is to define it, and all definition is
by limitation and exclusion; and that the only way to
say something distinct is to say something distinguishable; and distinguishable from everything else. In
short, I think that a man does not know what he is
saying until he knows what he is not saying.

At this moment, if we were to judge by a general
direction, by a vague unanimity existing in very vary-
ing degrees, and consisting of opinions rather similar
but not the same, we should certainly say there was a

universal wave of pacifism, just as in 1914 there was a general wave of patriotism. And when I say pacifism, I do not mean peace. It is possible, as I happen to know, to think pacifism a very direct menace to peace. But I am not debating these political points here. My thesis here is made up of very varied materials, and also of distinctly different views. Now, whatever we may think of those views, regarded as general political views, it will be well to pick out of them certain really preposterous propositions, as one would weed a patch of soil. Neither side of any controversy can be the better for mere confusion and delusion; still less for the confusion of one delusion with another, or of a delusion with a defensible opinion. There are many forms of pacifism which are quite defensible opinions, though I personally might be more inclined to attack than to defend them. There are any number of forms of peace policy which I should profoundly respect; and some with which I entirely agree. But one or two fancies have begun to form in the chaos which are simply fragments of fixed and frozen nonsense.

I have explained that I believe in drawing distinctions; or what is called splitting hairs. I do not believe in saying breezily that a fungus is pretty much the same as a fungoid, even if you are hungry and in a hurry to have mushrooms for breakfast; or agreeing heartily that a rhombus is the same as a rhomboid, because you have to hustle the geometricians in some plans for housing or surveying. I think the first sort of practicality will probably end with a number of people being poisoned with toadstools, or worse; and the latter with ungeometrical houses falling down on ungeometrical though practical men of action. And I wish to point out that you cannot conduct a policy of pacifism, or of anything else, unless you will consent to distinguish one idea from another; and to find out where your own ideas came from, and with what other ideas they conflict. This weeding of the weaker or wilder ideas out of the mind is simply a practical piece of gardening which applies to any sort of garden, even the garden of peace; even to a garden planted with nothing but olives, and undefiled with a single leaf of the laurel.

For instance, there is a wild hypothesis now hardening in the minds of many which has nothing to do with any philosophical case of pacifism, let alone peace. It is the notion that not fighting, as such, would prevent somebody else from fighting, or from taking all he wanted without fighting. It assumes that every pacifist is some strange sort of blend of a lion-tamer and a mesmerist, who would hold up invading armies with his glittering eye, like the Ancient Mariner. The pacifist would paralyse the militarist in all his actions, both militant and post-militant. Now, there is no sort of sense or even meaning in this notion at all. It is a muddle and mixture of a number of other and older pacific traditions, all of them much more reasonable and some of them quite right. Some of them are ancient attitudes of the saint or sage towards all sorts of misfortune; some of them are more or less mystical experiments in psychology, suitable to exceptional cases; some of them are mere dregs of dramatic or romantic situations, out of particular novels, plays, or short stories. There have been many great and good men in the past who have said that they would never need to resist spoliation or invasion, or would not care if it were irresistible. But they were almost always one of two types, and were thinking only of one or two truths. In some of them it meant: "My mind to me a kingdom is. The inner life is so deep and precious that I do not care if I am beggared or made an outlaw or even a slave." In the others it meant: "I know that my avenger liveth. The judgment of this world may beggar or enslave me, but I shall have justice when I appeal to a higher court." Both these moral attitudes mean something and something worthy of all possible respect. But neither of these two types was ever such a fool as to say that he *could* not be beggared or enslaved, merely because he stood stock still like a post and did not resist beggary or enslavement. Neither of them was so silly as to suppose that there were not men in the world, wicked or resolute or fanatical or mechanically servile enough, to do unpleasant things to them, while they were content to do nothing. The Stoic claimed to endure pain with patience; but he never claimed that his patience would prevent anybody from causing him pain. The martyr endured tortures to assert his belief in truth; but he never asserted

-{ 21 }-

his disbelief in torture. The hazy notion, that has been gathering more and more substance in the modern mind, is quite different and is really unreasonable. Men who have no intention of abandoning their country's wealth, not to mention their own, men who rightly insist on comfort for their countrymen and not infrequently for themselves, still seem to have formed a strange idea that they can keep all these things in all conceivable circumstances, solely and entirely by refusing to defend them. They seem to fancy they could bring the whole reign of violence and pride to an end, instantly and entirely, merely by doing nothing. Now it is not easy to do anything by doing nothing.

Oddly enough, the only exceptional hint of truth in this theory of establishing Peace is the same notion which made rude barbaric groups sometimes establish Trial by Battle. It was the notion that, under some very vivid and awful conditions, the man who knew he was in the wrong might lose his nerve. There was a story about that wicked man, Godwin the father of Harold, which illustrates the idea; and Scott used it as a dramatic turn in the death of the Templar. It did occasionally happen then; it might just conceivably happen now. But it happened because everybody believed in God, everybody thought the same about perjury and blasphemy, and a theory of justice was common to those who vindicated and those who violated it. In the present utter severance in fundamental ideas, I cannot see why even this exceptional trick should work at all. The pacifists are only a sect; and Europe is boiling over with equally sincere militarist and imperialist sects. Does anybody believe that Hitler or Stalin or Mussolini would ruin all his plans because a Quaker did not propose to interfere with them?

HISTORIANS will probably mark the present epoch by the problem of the Traffic. Unless, indeed, the historians, who are an absent-minded race of men, have all been killed by the traffic before they can write any histories of it. It seems an almost fitting fate for almost any literary man in such a chaos. I hope there is no irreverence to one of the most beautiful spiritual lyrics in the world if I say that that starry and blazing phrase of Francis Thompson, "Shall shine the traffic of Jacob's ladder pitched betwixt Heaven and Charing Cross," has sometimes raised in me an irrelevant wondering about whether a man could now safely fix his eyes on the angelic ladder in the middle of Charing Cross and its more earthly traffic; especially if he were a man like Francis Thompson. Anyhow, we are now primarily confronted with a problem of Traffic as Traffic; in the most ordinary meaning of the term. Social reformers of the last generation used the term as referring to the Drink Traffic; a little later there was a moral but slightly morbid panic about the White Slave Traffic; and the writers of detective stories, that blameless and industrious race, still frequently make their murders and mysteries turn upon the Drug Traffic. I may say, in passing, that I rather regret this re-

cent habit of criminological romancers. I like a murder
to be committed by a murderer for the serious moral
and spiritual reasons which make the murder immediately, though erroneously, satisfactory to his soul
and his inner life. I do not like to think that he is a
mere proletarian, dealing out poisons in the impersonal manner of a wholesale chemist. I dislike official
organization even in real life; and it is dreadful to
think of it invading romantic and imaginative life.
It is profoundly disappointing to suspect that somebody, let us say a curate or a governess, is torn with
seven devils of hate or pride or fear or envy; and then
discover that this promising demoniac is only a bright
and efficient salesman, receiving a commission for de-
livering the goods—if they can be so described. But
this is only a parenthesis, called forth by my permanent passion for the topic of detective stories. I only
mentioned the drug traffic in incidental comparison
with the driving traffic; and the latter has become a
problem quite as big and practically quite as deadly.

I am not going to propound here any practical solution for the traffic problem. I am not a rising politician; and not from my hand, or the waving of my
wand, will there ever arise all over London a new forest
of fantastic posts, surmounted by pumpkins or pine-
apples. But there is an inference from these things,
which is none the less practical because most practical
people will call it theoretical. Indeed, when matters are
in such a muddle as the modern traffic, the only really
practical thing is to find the right theory. Or, at any

rate, to be able to detect the wrong theory; and to form a general judgment upon how far a particular theory is right or wrong. When these difficulties first appeared, there was always a bustling, business-like person who went about cursing and swearing and saying that all that is wanted is organization. But in one sense it is easy enough to have organization, so long as you have obedience; and especially obedience to the police. But the limits of this theoretical truth can be seen at once if we pass from the case of policemen to the case of soldiers. There must be organization and obedience in an army. But battles are lost as well as won by concerted movements of disciplined troops. The question still remains in what order things are organized; or what orders men have to obey. In the traffic problem there are now complications of strategy that would have staggered Hannibal or Napoleon. But we are not yet certain whether they are part of a victory or a defeat. It is easy to organize traffic, by ordering that vehicles making the difficult advance from Piccadilly to Charing Cross had better make a detour round Hampstead Heath and turn up again somewhere in Cheapside. It is strictly systematic that every wheeled thing which is to pass from the Strand to Fleet Street should cross Waterloo Bridge, visit the charming suburbs of South London, look in on Croydon, and return triumphantly by the Tower Bridge. That is organization all right; bless its heart—and improve its head. But neither in military nor in social strategy is there much advantage in the unity and discipline that means making everybody make the same mistake at the same moment. The comment I would make is more casual and general; but it is not without its importance in other problems besides the problem of traffic.

Just now, for instance, it has a great deal to do with what may be called the problem of Progress. Many have accused people of my way of thinking of being merely hostile to Progress; especially in such scientific forms as petrol traffic. Many, but ill-acquainted with my habits, seem to suppose that I recoil in horror from a motor-car and insist on being wheeled about, like Mr. Pickwick, in a wheel-barrow. But that is not at all the part of Progress that I find problematical. I have no particular objection to people going about in cars; though I may regret the curious evolution of the human form in America, where wheels have completely taken the place of legs. What was not adequately realized, by those who merely talked about Progress, is simply this: that Progress is never merely the solving of problems, it is always also the setting of problems.

Men of the philosophic phase represented by Mr. H. G. Wells always tended to talk as if we should soon disentangle the knots of past problems merely by more science and experiment. What they did not see is that we are always tying new knots and making new tangles, actually because of science and experiment. Progress is the mother of Problems. I do not say that Progress is therefore undesirable; or that the problems are therefore insoluble. I only say there will always be numberless new problems to solve. Mr. Wells himself has uttered a magnificently defiant faith that his scientific Utopianism will win through and survive the reaction against it all over Europe; because, as he says, intelligence cannot ultimately be defeated. I might say, in passing, that I see no purely rationalist proof that intelligence cannot be defeated. And I should rather like to know who decides that Mussolini and Maurras of the *Action Française* are unintelligent. But the point at the moment is that men like Mr. Wells did talk as if Progress would be so intelligent as to relieve us of one problem after another; and did not allow enough for the fact that Progress itself might add yet another problem. We may, as a scientific prophet lately said, fly to the stars; though I for one find the earth far more mysterious. But if we do fly to the stars, there will be a traffic problem about flying-ships, exactly as there is now a traffic problem about taxicabs.

That is perhaps the most lasting lesson of the petrol traffic problem. The problem may disappear. The petrol traffic may disappear. But meanwhile we pass through what is a nightmare of mere nonsense; everybody made to have motor-horns; everybody forbidden to use motor-horns; everybody going round in circles as something straighter than a straight line; all the utter unreason of the mind when fronted with a riddle that seems insoluble. By all means go on progressing, if it amuses you; go on inventing machines for anything or everything. But always remember that you are not only inventing machines; you are inventing riddles.

Few people, I fancy, can feel very happy about motoring conditions in this country of late; unless it be in the rather curious sense which Matthew Arnold attributed to Goethe, in a very obvious imitation of Virgil:

> And he was happy, if to know
> Causes of things and far below
> His feet to see the insensate flow
> Of folly and insane distress
> And headlong fate, be happiness.

The above lines embody a very exact discription of the condition of motoring on our roads during recent years. There has been plenty of folly and headlong fate; and not a little insane distress and, what is perhaps more terrible, entirely sane distress. But I doubt if even the most detached could regard the contemplation of it as a condition of happiness. Nevertheless, I confess that I have a fancy for thinking about the causes of things; if I may presume so far to put myself in the company of Virgil or Goethe or Matthew Arnold. For the rest, I am not a motorist or a motor, or one specially to be described by any term indicating rapid or frequent motion. I am not enough of a traveller to find that traffic problem a very pressing problem; still less the problem which is not so much the motion as the stopping of traffic. In fact, I fear I never like the traffic quite so much as when it stands still. In the middle of a prolonged block in the Uxbridge Road, I have been known to exhibit a gaiety and radiant levity which has made me loathed and detested for miles round. I always feel a faint hope, after a few hours of it, that the vehicles may never move on at all; but may sink slowly into the road and take on the more rooted character of a large and prosperous village. Perhaps, after all, it is thus that our culture may return to the stability and sanity of the earth, which is now its only hope. I have sometimes felt inclined to get out of the car and make a little garden just outside it, staking out a claim and symbolically renouncing all hope of any further advance.

ALL my life long the noise of battle rolled, chiefly between dramatic critics and theatrical managers, about
the rights and wrongs of the Censorship of Plays; and
I have no doubt the noise is still going on over any cor-
responding Censorship of Films. But though there
were incessant differences between those who agreed
with the Censor and those who disagreed with him,
none of the differences were so great as the difference
between two reasons for disagreeing. There were some
who seemed to hold that any artistic experiment, however anarchical or abnormal, or manifestly and even
medically insane, had a mysterious right of its own
to override any social custom or convenience, any
common-sense or ordinary civic dignity. The artistic
experiment had this right because it was an artistic
experiment; not even because the art was artistic; still
less because the experiment was successful. Even the
worst play must take precedence of the best law. If
the artists had wanted to have real blood in their murders, as some other artists used real mud on their land-
scapes, one can only suppose that these critics would
have agreed to sacrifice a few human lives to the thrill
of realism. If the actor-manager were working on the
old lavish scale, he might be encouraged to turn the

theatre into an amphitheatre. He might make a feature of real lions, which would be expensive; and real Christians, who would be rare.

Anyhow, the theory of the thing seemed to be that supreme spiritual authority in this world belongs to art, or rather, to anybody who chooses to say that he is attempting something new in art. I was never able to accept this highly modern and credulous conception; because I am unable to imagine any human being accepting any authority that he has not originally reached by reason. And I cannot conceive what reason there could possibly be for accepting the authority of artists; not to mention bad artists. But it was a very common attitude thirty or forty years ago; and it covers large spaces of society still. There is a great deal that is amusing about this arbitrary sort of artist, as well as the more obvious joke of his art. Perhaps the funniest thing of all about him is that he sometimes calls himself a Pagan. He is the sort of man who might be murdered almost anywhere, even in an English Socialist revolution; but if there is one place where he would be killed quite instantly for defying the gods and disregarding the dignity of the republic, it is in a city of the Pagans.

But there always was, and there still is, an exactly contrary case against the Censor and the Censorship. It is that the rules of the Censorship encourage anarchy, and that the worst sort of anarchy, which is anarchy in the mind. There is an obvious example, which I mentioned long ago, when this debate was more topical. By the old rule of Censorship, we must not put Jesus on the stage. It would be much easier to put Judas on the stage. It would be perfectly easy to justify Judas on the stage. There is now no form of blasphemy or bad morals that anybody is really forbidden to justify on the stage. A modern drama may be one wild dance of all the devils and all the swine. It may contain anything or anybody, except anybody who can cast out devils or destroy swine. Generally speaking, in the whole spirit of the thing, the one thing that the Censor can really cut out is God. He has no particular reason to cut out Satan; and no reason at all to cut out Satanism. No doubt the actual wielders of such powers try to soften their insane regulations by behaving as sanely as they can. But I am not talking about the Censor, but about the rules of the Censorship. And though they are by this time an old example, they are still perhaps the most distinct and disputable example of a certain moral muddle into which this country has managed to stumble during the last half-century. One other example is "Divorce Law Reform." One may think Divorce wrong; and yet feel it almost worse if men cannot even do wrong without a tangle of quibbles and lies.

Now, since the days when the Censorship quarrel existed in that form, the whole social situation has changed. I was about to say that much water has flowed under the bridges; but it would perhaps be truer to say that it has flowed over the bridges and overwhelmed the world with a flood. In those earlier days to which I have just referred, there was any amount of the artistic revolt and riot I have just described. But the revolt of artists was almost entirely a revolt of artists; or, rather, of a minority of artists. There was also, as I have said, a still smaller minority of those who rebelled, as I did, not so much because we revered art as because we respected reason. But all the rest of the people, that is the overwhelming majority of the people, were still traditional in their ethics though rather vague in their religion. Allowing for all exaggeration, we may fairly say of the new generation that it is the ethics that are vague; except in certain cases where they are decidedly vivid. And a real problem arises, about what we should do, in face of such a change of proportion even in the vague moral opinion of modern society. When I say a problem, I do not in the least mean what is meant by a doubt. I do not mean that I have a shadow of doubt about what we personally should do; and especially what we should not do. We should not do as they do; any more than we should beat Jews because we are in Prussia, or murder priests because we are in Mexico. There is no question of doubt about what is right for us to do, or to say; it is rather a question of what it is possible for us to prevent. Now, I think those who hold the old view of right should stand firm, stand apart and even realize they stand alone. They should attack. England looks much more hopeful as a Pagan country calling for conversion than as a Christian country calling for compromise. The roast beef of Old England will last longer when it is salted beef. But if the salt lose its savour, wherewith shall it be salted?

We may fall back on the historic base of modern progress, on the fundamentals not yet formally reversed; and there is a case for it. We might say that if six undiscovered murders this year become sixty undiscovered murders next year, the commonwealth none the less rests on the idea that murder is wrong. We may say that three thieves to-day and thirty to-morrow and three hundred the day after to-morrow do not turn us into a Communist society. On the other hand, we may admit that, though not a Communist society, it is no longer a Christian society. And then, if we are Christians, we can launch a crusade to convert or conquer it. Now I think, after some sincere thought, that this latter course is by far the better. I do not believe in ignoring the Pagan morals all around us: it does not diminish the Paganism; and it only deprives us of the pleasure and advantage of denouncing it as Pagan. The assumption that tradition, and even convention, that virtue and even Victorian virtue, is still the rule, and anything else an exception, is all on the side of the sophists who defend vice. It is a rule by which we carry all the unpopular emblems of power, while they enjoy all the practical fruits of victory. They can flout us, because they profess that there is nothing to conceal; and we cannot fight them, because we pretend that there is nothing to fight. But, above all, from the point of the honest orthodox, the present one-sided truce has this enormous disadvantage: it prevents us from pointing out the one solid, staring, stupendous fact which is before all our eyes. It is the fact that we have not only seen a modern materialist civilization rise, but we have seen it fall. We have seen industrial imperialism and individualism a *practical* failure. It is no longer a question of using the modern machinery; but of cutting loose from the wreck of it.

THERE are some who actually like the Country dialects which State education is systematically destroying. There are some who actually prefer them to the Cockney dialect which State education is systematically spreading. For that is perhaps the most practical and successful effect of our present scheme of public instruction, that the village children no longer talk like ignorant inhabitants of Sussex or Suffolk; they now talk like enlightened inhabitants of Hoxton and Houndsditch. Among the eccentric reactionaries who have actually observed this change with regret, a further and more curious fact has also been remarked more than once. An Anglican country parson, a friend of mine, once told me that it was not only a loss of pronunciation, but also of perception. "They not only can't say the word, but they can't hear it," was the way he put it. Supposing that the virtuous vicar in question had been so ill-advised as to teach his infant school to recite, let us say, the "Dolores" of Swinburne—which, I admit, is not extremely probable—their intonation would be different, but without any intention to differ. The vicar would say, "Ringed round with a flame of fair faces." And the Sunday School children would obediently repeat, "Ringed

rarnd with a flime of fair fices," with a solid certainty
and assurance that this was exactly what he had said.
However laboriously he might entreat them to say
"faces," they would say "fices," and it would sound
to them exactly like "faces."

In short, this sort of thing is not a variation or a
form of variety; on the contrary, it is an inability to
see that there is any variety. It is not a difference in the
sense of a distinction; on the contrary, it is a sudden
failure in the power to make any distinction. Whatever
is distinct may possibly be distinguished. And Burns
and Barnes did manage to be distinguished, in the
particular form of distinction commonly called dialect. But the change here in question is something
much more formless and much more formidable than
anything that could arise from the most uncouth or
unlucky of local or rustic accents. It is a certain loss of
sharpness, in the ear as well as the tongue; not only a
flattening of the speech, but a deadening of the hearing. And though it is in itself a relatively small matter, especially as compared with many parallel matters, it is exactly this quality that makes it symbolic
in the social problems of to-day. For one of the deepest
troubles of the day is this fact: that something is being
commended as a new taste which is simply the condition which finds everything tasteless. It is sometimes
offered almost as if it were a new sense; but it is not
really even a new sensibility; it is rather a pride in a
new insensibility.

For instance, when some old piece of decorum is

abolished, rightly or wrongly, it is always supposed
to be completely justified if people become just as dull
in accepting the indecency as they were in accepting
the decency. If it can be said that the grandchildren
"soon get used" to something that would have made
the grandfathers fight duels to the death, it is always
assumed that the grandchildren have found a new
mode of living, whereas those who fought the duel to
the death were already dead. But the psychological
fact is exactly the other way. The duellists may have
been fastidious or even fantastic, but they were frightfully alive. That is why they died. Their sensibilities
were vivid and intense, by the only true test of the
finer sensibilities, or even of the five senses. And that
is that they could feel the difference between one thing
and another. It is the livelier eye that can see the difference between peacock-blue and peacock-green; it is
the more fatigued eye that may see them both as
something very like grey. It is the quicker ear that
can detect in any speech the shade between innocence
and irony, or between irony and insult. It is the duller
ear that hears all the notes as monotone, and therefore
monotonous. Even the swaggering person, who was
supposed to turn up his nose at everything, was at least
in a position to sniff the different smells of the world,
and perhaps to detect their difference.

There is the drearier and more detached sort of pride
of the other sort of man, who may be said to turn his
nose down at everything. For that also is only a more
depressing way of turning everything down. It is not

a mark of purity of taste, but of absence of taste, to think that cocoa is as good as claret; and in the field of morals it may well have the ultimate Nemesis of thinking cocaine as good as cocoa. Even the mere senses, in the merely sensual sense, attest to this truth about vivacity going with differentiation. It is no answer, therefore, to say that you have persuaded a whole crowd of hygienic hikers to be content with cocoa any more than to say that you have persuaded a whole crowd of drug-fiends to be content with cocaine. Neither of them is the better for pursuing a course which spoils the palate, and probably robs them of a reasonable taste in vintages. But what most modern people do not see is that this dullness in diet, and similar things, is exactly parallel to the dull and indifferent anarchy in manners and morals. Do not be proud of the fact that your grandmother was shocked at something which you are accustomed to seeing or hearing without being shocked. There are two meanings of the word "nervous," and it is not even a physical superiority to be actually without nerves. It may mean that your grandmother was an extremely lively and vital animal, and that you are a paralytic.

We are constantly told, for instance, by the very prosaic paralytics who call themselves Nudists, that people "soon get used" to being degraded, in that particular, to the habits of the beasts of the field. I have no doubt they do; just as they soon get used to being drunkards or drug-fiends or jail-birds or people talking Cockney instead of talking English. Where the argument of the apologist entirely fails is in showing that it is *better* to get used to an inferior status after losing a superior one. In a hundred ways, recent legislation has ridden roughshod over the instincts of innocent and simple and yet very sensible people. There was a feeling, strangely enough, that men and women might not feel very comfortable when they met as total strangers to discuss some depraved and perhaps disgusting aspect of their natural sex relation. This has already given a good deal of quiet trouble on juries, and we have not seen the end of the trouble yet. Now, it will be noted that the objection to female juries never was an objection to juries being female. There always were female juries. From the first days of legislation a number of matrons were empanelled to decide certain points among each other. The case against mixed juries was a case of embarrassment; and that embarrassment is far more intelligent, far more civilized, far more subtle, far more psychological than the priggish brutality that disregards it. But, in any case, it will serve here as an illustration of what I mean. The question is not whether the embarrassment can be so far overcome somehow that a good many people can discharge the duty somehow. The question is whether the blunting of the sentiment really is a victory for human culture, and not rather a defeat for human culture. Just as the question is not whether millions of little boys, in different districts with different dialects, can all be taught the same dialect of the Whitechapel Road, but whether that dialect is better than others; and whether it is a good thing to lose the sense of difference between dialects.

For what we do at least know, in the most fundamental fashion, is that man is man by the possession of these fastidious fancies; from which the free-thinking haddock is entirely emancipated, and by which the latitudinarian turnip is never troubled. To lose the sense of repugnance from one thing, or regard for another, is exactly so far as it goes to relapse into the vegetation or to return to the dust. But for about fifty or sixty years nearly all our culture and controversial trend has been conducted on the assumption that, as long as we could get used to any sort of caddishness, we could be perfectly contented in being cads. I do not say that all the results of the process have been wrong. But I do say that the test of the process has been wrong from first to last; for it is not a case against the citizen that a man can grow *accustomed* to being either a savage or a slave.

In dealing with such things as Prohibition, I have sometimes had occasion to mention Puritanism. Disputes have arisen about this word, and about how far it is fair to associate it at least with a mild shade of pessimism. Sporadic attempts are made to modify this strong popular impression; and I saw an article the other day which largely turned upon a statement that Calvin was allowed to play with darts. As I have not the least desire to be unfair to Puritans, I think I should like to sum up what seems to me the substantial historical truth of the matter, and the real point of the whole story. So far as I am concerned, the point is not so much against Calvin as against Calvinism; and not so much even against Calvinism as against that much less logical Modernism which has taught everybody in our time that religious error does not matter. It matters very much in two ways; and Puritanism is a striking historical example of both. First: something that might well seem to sensible people to be only a fine shade of thought, merely theoretical and theological, does, in fact, change the mind. It produces a mood which does darken the world, or some particular part of the world. About

the degree of the darkness or the density of the
cloud, we may well differ; but it is a matter of
common sense to see where the cloud did or does
rest. Nobody will dare to maintain that the Scottish Sabbath has not in fact been more strict
than the English Sunday, let alone the Continental
Sunday. Every one knows that it was the Puritans
who objected to Archbishop Laud's famous publication on the subject; every one knows that
they objected to his Book of Sports because
it was a book of sports; every one knows that they
thought the sports too sportive. Attempts to
explain away solid outstanding historical facts of
this kind are altogether fanciful. But it does not
follow that every founder of every sect involved
attached supreme importance to this particular
point; some of them did; some of them did not.
The whole movement grew gradually from various
roots, but this is what it grew to be. A man alive
in the middle of the Renaissance, speculating about
a system of Presbyters which he had not yet begun
to found, amid a thousand others speculating
about a thousand other things, would not, of course,
become instantly identical with a Presbyterian
minister of modern times. He would not begin
on the spot to grow the black top-hat and bushy
whiskers of a Scottish elder or precentor in one of
Sir James Barrie's plays or stories. *Nemo repente
fit turpissimus.* Which it would doubtless be very
unfair to translate as "No one suddenly becomes a

precentor."

But there is another historical process involved. It is much more curious, and it has been much more curiously neglected. One special form of the harm done by the extreme sects in the seventeenth century was this: that they really died young, and that what has infected our culture since has not been their life, or even their death, but rather their decay. In most cases the Puritans lost their religion and retained their morality; a deplorable state of things for anybody. If the special narrow theologies had not perished as rapidly as they did, the atmospheric moral mood would not have lingered on exactly in the way it did. But, above all, it permitted of a process which seems to me one of the strangest and most interesting in human history, but does not seem as yet to have been noticed by historians. It is rather like the geological process of the formation of a fossil. Every one knows that a fossil fish is not a fish; nor a fossil bird a bird. I do not mean merely in the obvious sense; that we should be surprised —nay, annoyed—in a restaurant, if we asked for a fish and they gave us a stone. I mean that a fossil is a form in which remains no actual fragment of a fish. It in a hollow mould or image of a fish, which is very gradually filled up by the infiltration of something else, after the actual fish has decayed. Thus we find the general outline of these stony and very literal faiths filled up by something else when the old fanaticism has decayed. There are two great modern examples of that creepy and uncanny historical transmutation. One is what we call Prohibition, and the other is what we call Prussianism.

The point is perhaps clearest in the case of Prohibition. The old original Puritans were not Prohibitionists. Oliver Cromwell was a brewer; but he was not inspired or intoxicated by beer, nor (like the teetotallers) inspired and intoxicated by the absence of beer. Whatever his faults, he did most certainly have a real religion, in the sense of a creed. But it was a sombre creed, one which had been made intentionally more stern and ruthless than the other creeds; and this created a new mood and moral atmosphere which ultimately spread all over the great plains of Puritan America. Now, the point is this: that as the creed crumbled slowly as a creed, its place was taken by something vaguer but of the same general spirit. The sombre theological system was replaced by a sombre social theory. You can put it another way if you like, and say that America tolerated Prohibition; not because America was Puritan, but because America had been Puritan. The idea of morality that came to prevail till lately at least was in every sense a survival of Puritanism, even if it was also in a sense a substitute for Puritanism. That is the essential history of that curious episode; the teetotal ethic of modern times. Prohibition was not a part of the origin of Puritanism; none the less, Prohibition was a thing of Puritan origin.

The same is true of the religious fanaticism that filled Germany in the Thirty Years War; as compared with the national or tribal fanaticism that now fills Germany after the Great War. The old fanatics who followed Gustavus Adolphus and William of Orange were not ethnologists or evolutionists. They did not imagine that they belonged to a Nordic Race; they most certainly did not imagine that they or theirs had ever been bothered with a Swastika. They saluted the cross or they smashed the cross; but it had not occurred to them to tap the four ends of it so as to turn it into a fragment of Chinese or Red Indian decoration. They were thinking about their own strictly religious scruples and schisms. They were really fighting fiercely and savagely for points of doctrine; and I should be the last to blame them for it. But those doctrines did not last; they were the very doctrines that have now long been dissolving in the acids of German scepticism, in the laboratories of the Prussian professors. And the more they evaporated and left a void, the more the void was filled up with new and boiling elements; with tribalism, with militarism, with imperialism, and (in short) with that very narrow type of patriotism that we call Prussianism.

Most of us would agree that this kind of patriotism is a considerable peril to every other kind of patriotism. That is the whole evil of the ethno-logical type of loyalty. Settled States can respect themselves and also respect each other, because they can claim the right to defend their own fron-tiers and yet not deny their duty to recognize other people's frontiers. But the racial spirit is a restless spirit; it does not go by frontiers but by the wandering of the blood. It is not so much as if France were at war with Spain, but rather as if the Gipsies were more or less at war with everybody. You can have a League of Nations, but you could hardly have a League of Tribes. When the Tribe is on the march, it is apt to forget leagues—not to mention frontiers. But my immediate interest in this flood of tribalism is that it has since poured into the empty hollows left by the slow drying-up of the great Deluge of the Thirty Years War; and that all this new and naked nationalism has come to many modern men as a substitute for their dead religion.

PERHAPS the quaint old tradition that the village cobbler is always the village atheist may have had something to do with the equally quaint old proverb that the cobbler should stick to his last. *Ne sutor ultra crepidam* may have been a pagan proverb; but an atheist was probably as rare among polytheists as he is among monotheists. And it seems rather to suggest a mild complaint among customers that their favourite expert in footwear was rather neglecting their feet in his irrelevant efforts to influence their heads. And whereas their feet might have been shod with the gospel of peace, by a more pious and traditional cobbler, it was found that their heads were turned into watch-towers loud with the tocsins and alarums of war, by the challenges of the atheistic cobbler. It may seem at first a little hard on the cobbler to condemn him to an eternal ritual of repeating that there is nothing like leather. But there is a truly historic half-truth in the idea of such a limitation. And the truth is this: that a really good cobbler might be really interesting about leather, and still be capable of being rather a bore about God; and still more of a bore about

Godlessness. And the reason is this: that in the trade that a man really understands he often has ideas that are really his own; he is fresh and inventive and even (in the rare but good sense) up to date.

Whereas, in a theoretical thing like atheism, he is almost certain to have picked up stale ideas that are not his own; that are not even in the vulgar sense up to date; that are generally likely to be all the more ancient because he fancies they are modern. A true craftsman of St. Crispin, a great and glorious cobbler in the best tradition of the Guilds, might mean much more than we imagine in saying that there is nothing like leather. He might be thinking that leather is not one thing but a thousand things; that he himself had a score of schemes for the extension and variation of its use; that the world was only at the beginning of the vast possibilities and scientific applications of leather. He might see in a vision, not only the forest of the fantastic elongations of the late mediæval shoe, but all the other historic applications that still live in legend; from the Leather Bottel to the complete costume of leather that was worn by the first Quaker. He might see new shapes cut out of leather, new patterns stamped on leather, new ways in which the use of leather might extend from hats to hangings, curtains or carpets, as the use of lead extends from bullets to church windows. If he had these new notions about leather, it would be largely because he had studied leather, and not stuck behind in the first alphabet of his craft. But as an atheist he would be an amateur, and would probably have stuck very stupidly at the first alphabet of atheism; asking how the God who made a fig tree grow could stop it from growing; or whether God was not alone responsible for all a man did, because he had made a man free to do what he liked. Anyhow, he would probably say things we have all heard a thousand times from cosmic theorists, and do not specially want to hear all over again from cobblers.

Certainly no one would compare Sir James Jeans to an atheist; for no man has, in fact, done more to change the tone of the most modern science from atheism to theism. Nor would it be strictly correct, or in accordance with the dull details of biography as given in *Who's Who,* to describe him as a cobbler. But in one way he does raise some of the same questions as are suggested in the two proverbs about the cobbler, or the faintly implied speculations about the atheist. I was listening recently to conversations which still continue about a recent lecture of Sir James Jeans to the British Association, not to mention the echoes of it that still rumble in the popular Press. And I was struck in both these cases, especially in the case of the newspapers, with the much greater space and attention given to his general peroration about science in relation to ethics and politics and religion

(about which studies he is, after all, an amateur
like the rest of us), than to the masterly analysis
of his own original ideas about matter of the
mathematics of energy, about which he is possibly
the chief authority of the age. The cosmic cobbler
is listened to less respectfully when he talks about
leather, about the substance or material of which
the cosmos is made, than when he talks about the
problem of unemployment or armament, or the
need of a new religion, or all the familiar topics
well within the range of the village atheist, or at
least of the village agnostic. And yet his hypothesis
about matter is full of new ideas, which are really
his own; while his defence of the morality of modern
science is necessarily full of old ideas which would
have been much the same in the mouths of the
scientific men of sixty years ago.

Nor, indeed, are they altogether satisfactory, and
they have become rather less so by mere repetition,
in a world that has been revolutionized in the
interval. No religious person, unless he is a religious maniac, has any particular reason to resist the
advance of physical science; least of all the physical
science of the new physicists. But since Sir James
goes out of his way to counter or contradict the
evil that has accompanied the good, we may fairly
point out that the contradiction is not a refutation.
The harnessing of science to hellish engines of
destruction has not grown better, because a great
deal of blood has flown under the bridges since

old Huxley idealized the social use of science. And to say that if machinery creates unemployment it also creates new industries and new employment, is simply to be stone blind to the staring and outstanding fact of the hour. That fact is that, even allowing for every effort to make new industries, unemployment has, on the balance, enormously increased. And this particular defence of machinery is so very far from being new that it would have sounded very much more true if it had been made (as it was made) in the middle of the nineteenth century, during the triumph of the Manchester manufacturers. In those Early Victorian days, it really was much more arguable that we were putting as many men into new enterprises as we were throwing out of old ones. To-day it is not true at all, as a matter of the facts and even the statistics. But, anyhow, we do not go to the most brilliant scientist of our own time to hear things that might be excused in an Early Victorian.

Or, again, in a man of so much scientific originality, there is the same strange staleness in the statement that we must make a modern religion to suit modern scientific knowledge. Here he seems to forget, not only all that has been done since the age of dogmatic materialism, but even all that he has done himself. He seems strangely oblivious of the actual nature of that "knowledge" which he has just been revealing in his own lecture.

For, according to his own vivid and fascinating description, that knowledge largely consists of a sort of radiant and luminous ignorance. The whole point of his address was that he had come to the conclusion that something, in the very nature of our observance of phenomena, forbids us to feel sure that it is the ultimate fact which we observe. Whether this be true or no, it is surely not the sort of truth of which anybody could make a religion; or on which we could build any system of sacrifice or confidence or obedience. There was at least some sense in Haeckel and the old materialists saying that we must fit our moral philosophy to the facts. But why should we fit it to a fancy-picture of the cosmos, that may have hardly any relation to the facts? If it points to anything, it would seem to point back to the old idea that, if we really want a religion, we must seek it with our own reason, with our moral convictions and our conception of the metaphysics of being. But if men could not find faith among the atoms of which they were sure, they will hardly find it among the electrons of which they are not sure. But my main purpose is merely to protest against the treatment of this great man of science by the world of journalism and gossip, which thinks him so much more important when he happens to use a few familiar phrases from the old freethinkers than when his phraseology is really unfamiliar and his thought is really free.

ALL Christian history began with that great social occasion when Pilate and Herod shook hands. Hitherto, as everybody knew in Society circles, they had hardly been on speaking terms. Something led them to seek each other's support, a vague sense of social crisis, though very little was happening except the execution of an ordinary batch of criminals. The two rulers were reconciled on the very day when one of these convicts was crucified. That is what many people mean by Peace, and the substitution of a reign of Love for one of Hatred. Whether or no there is honour among thieves, there is always a certain social interdependence and solidarity among murderers; and those sixteenth-century ruffians who conspired to assassinate Rizzio or Darnley were always very careful to put their names, and especially each other's names, to what they called a "band," so that at the worst they might all hang together. Many political friendships—nay, even broad democratic comradeships, are of this nature; and their representatives are really distressed when we decline to identify this form of Love with the original mystical idea of Charity.

It sometimes seems to me that history is dominated and determined by these evil friendships. As all Christian history begins with the happy reconciliation of Herod and Pilate, so all modern history, in the recent revolutionary sense, begins with that strange friendship which ended in a quarrel, as the first quarrel had ended in a friendship. I mean that the two elements of destruction, which make the modern world more and more incalculable, were loosened with the light of that forgotten day when a lean French gentleman in a large wig, by name M. Arouet, travelled north with much annoyance to find the palace of a Prussian King far away in the freezing Baltic plain. The strict title of the King in dynastic chronicles is Frederick the Second, but he is better known as Frederick the Great. The actual name of the Frenchman was Arouet, but he is better known as Voltaire. The meeting of these two men, in the mid-winter of eighteenth-century scepticism and secularism, is a sort of spiritual marriage which brought forth the modern world; *monstrum horrendum, informe, ingens, cui lumen ademptum.* But because that birth was monstrous and evil, and because true friendship and love are not evil, it did not come into the world to create one united thing, but two conflicting things, which, between them, were to shake the world to pieces. From Voltaire the Latins were to learn a raging scepticism. From Frederick the Teutons were to learn a raging pride.

We may note at the start that neither of them cared very much about his own country or traditions. Frederick was a German who refused even to learn German. Voltaire was a Frenchman who wrote a foul lampoon about Joan of Arc. They were cosmopolitans; they were not in any sense patriots. But there is this difference; that the patriot does, however stupidly, like the country: whereas the cosmopolitan does not in the least like the cosmos. They neither of them pretended to like anything very much. Voltaire was the more really humane of the two; but Frederick also could talk on occasion the cold humanitarianism that was the cant of his age. But Voltaire, even at his best, really began that modern mood that has blighted all the humanitarianism he honestly supported. He started the horrible habit of helping human beings only through pitying them, and never through respecting them. Through him the oppression of the poor became a sort of cruelty to animals, and the loss of all that mystical sense that to wrong the image of God is to insult the ambassador of a King.

Nevertheless, I believe that Voltaire had a heart; I think that Frederick was most heartless when he was most humane. Anyhow, these two great sceptics met on the level, on the dead solid plain, as dull as the Baltic Plain; on the basis that there is no God, or no God who is concerned with men any more than with mites in cheese. On this basis they agreed; on this basis they disagreed; their quarrel was personal and trivial, but it ended by launching two European forces against each other, both rooted in the same unbelief. Voltaire said in effect: "I will show you that the sneers of a sceptic can produce a Revolution and a Republic and everywhere the overthrowing of thrones." And Frederick answered: "And I will show you that this same sneering scepticism can be used as easily to resist Reform, let alone Revolution; that scepticism can be the basis of support for the most tyrannical of thrones, for the bare brute domination of a master over his slaves." So they said farewell, and have since been sundered by two centuries of war; they said farewell, but presumably did not say "adieu."

Of every such evil seed it may be noted that the seed is different from the flower, and the flower from the fruit. A demon of distortion always twists it even out of its own unnatural nature. It may turn into almost anything, except anything really good. It is, to use the playful term of affection which Professor Freud applies to his baby, "a polymorphous pervert." These things not only do not produce the special good they promise; they do not produce even the special evil they threaten. The Voltairean revolt promised to produce, and even began to produce, the rise of mobs and overthrow of thrones; but it was not the final form of scepticism. The actual effect of what we call democracy has been the disappearance of the mob. We might say there were mobs at the beginning of the Revolution and no mobs at the end of it. That Voltairean influence has not ended in the rule of mobs, but in the rule of secret societies. It has falsified politics throughout the Latin world, till the recent Italian Counter-Revolution. Voltaire has produced hypocritical and pompous professional politicians, at whom he would have been the first to jeer. But on his side, as I have said, there does linger a certain humane and civilized sentiment which is not unreal. Only it is right to remember what has really gone wrong on his side of the Continental quarrel when we are recording the much wilder and wickeder wrong on the other side of it.

For the evil spirit of Frederick the Great has produced, not only all other evils, but what might seem the very opposite evil. He who worshipped nothing has become a god who is quite blindly worshipped. He who cared nothing for Germany has become the battle-cry of madmen who care for nothing except Germany. He who was a cold cosmopolitan has heated seven times a hell of narrow national and tribal fury which at this moment menaces mankind with a war that may be the end of the world. But the root of both perversions is in the common ground of atheist irresponsibility; there was nothing to stop the sceptic from turning democracy into secrecy; there was nothing to stop him interpreting liberty as the infinite licence of tyranny. The spiritual zero of Christendom was at that freezing instant when those two dry, thin, hatchet-faced men looked in each other's hollow eyes and saw the sneer that was as eternal as the smile of a skull. Between them, they have nearly killed the thing by which we live.

These two points of peril or centres of unrest, the intellectual unrest of the Latins and the very unintellectual unrest of the Teutons, do doubtless both contribute to the instability of international relations, and threaten us all the more because they threaten each other. But when we have made every allowance for there being, in that sense, dangers on both sides, the main modern fact emerges that the danger is mostly on one side, and that we have long been taught to look for it only on the other side. Much of Western opinion, especially English and American, has been trained to have a vague horror of Voltaire, often combined with a still vaguer respect for Frederick. No Wesleyans are likely to confuse Wesley with Voltaire. No Primitive Methodist is under the impression that Voltaire was a Primitive Methodist. But many such Protestant ministers really were under the impression that Frederick the Great was a Protestant Hero. None of them realized that Frederick was the greater atheist of the two. None of them certainly foresaw that Frederick, in the long run, would turn out to be the greater anarchist of the two. In short, nobody foresaw what everybody afterwards saw: the French Republic becoming a conservative force, and the Prussian Kingdom a purely destructive and lawless force. Victorians like Carlyle actually talked about pious Prussia, as if Blücher had been a saint or Moltke a mystic. General Göring may be trusted to teach us better, till we learn at last that nothing is so anarchical as discipline divorced from authority; that is, from right.

SOME time ago, when a stir was made by a rather striking book called *Who Moved the Stone?* which might almost be described, with all reverence, as a divine detective story and almost a theological thriller, a pugnacious little paper in Fleet Street made a remark which has always hovered in my memory as more mysterious than any mystery story in the world. The writer said that any man who believes in the Resurrection is bound to believe also in the story of Aladdin in the *Arabian Nights.* I have no idea what he meant. Nor, I imagine, had he. But this curious conjunction of ideas recurs to my mind in connexion with a rather interesting suggestion made by Mr. Christopher Dawson about what we may call the History of Science. On the face of it, the remark I have quoted from the pugnacious paper seems to have no quality whatever except pugnacity. There is no sort of logical connexion between believing in one marvellous event and believing in another, even if they were exactly alike and not utterly different. If I believe that Captain Peary reached the North Pole, I am not therefore bound to believe that Dr. Cook also reached the North Pole, even if they both arrived with sledges and dogs out of the same snows. It is a fallacy, therefore, even where the two things are close enough to be compared. But the comparison between the Gospel miracle and the Arabian fairy-tale is about the most unfortunate comparison in the world. For in the one case there is a plain and particular reason for thinking the thing true, or at least meant to be true. And in the other case there is a plain and particular reason for realizing that the tale is not only untrue, but is not even meant to be true.

The historical case for the Resurrection is that everybody else, except the Apostles, had every possible motive to declare what they had done with the body, if anything had been done with it. The Apostles might have hidden it in order to announce a sham miracle, but it is very difficult to imagine men being tortured and killed for the truth of a miracle which they knew to be a sham. In the case of the Apostles' testimony, the general circumstances suggest that it is true. In the case of the Arabian tale, the general circumstances avow and proclaim that it is false. For we are told in the book itself that all the stories were told by a woman merely to amuse the king and distract his attention from the idea of cutting off her head. A romancer in this personal situation is not very likely to confine herself strictly to humdrum accuracy, and it would be impossible more plainly to warn the reader that all the tales are taradiddles.

In the one case, then, we have witnesses who not only think the thing true, but do veritably think it is as true as death, or truer than death. They therefore prefer death to the denial of its truth. In the other case we have a story-teller who, in trying to avoid death, has every motive to tell lies. If St. John the Baptist had wished to avoid being beheaded, and had saved his life by inventing a long string of Messianic or Early Christian legends on the spur of the moment, in order to hold the attention of King Herod, I should not regard any "resurrection myth" he might tell as a strong historical argument for the Resurrection. But, as the Apostles were killed as St. John was killed, I think their evidence cannot be identified by sound scholarship as a portion of the Arabian Nights.

I merely pause for a moment upon this wild and preposterous parallel as a passing example of the queer way in which sceptics now refuse to follow an argument and only follow a sort of association or analogy. But the real reason for recalling this strange remark about the Arabian Nights is to be found in a much more genuine analogy between Western Science and Eastern Sorcery. Nobody but a lunatic would look either for his facts or his faith in the Arabian Nights. But, oddly enough, there really was a touch of the Arabian magicians in the Arabian mathematicians. There really was a faint flavour of the Oriental wizardry about the quite genuine Oriental wisdom; even when that wisdom was really doing work for which the world will always be grateful, in geometry or chemistry, in mathematics or medicine. Thus we find the paradox: that a man might, after all, look for some of the elements of science in the Arabian Nights, though he would hardly look there for anything very edifying or elevating in the way of the elements of religion. In short, the old dim, or even dark, connexion between Medicine and Magic has a sort of hidden meaning of great historical interest. It is developed by Mr. Dawson in an essay on the Eastern element in early mediæval science, and occurs in a book of essays called *Mediæval Religion*.

But this particular point is not concerned with religion, but is connected in a curious way with science. The point is this: that Magic (in the ancient sense) and Medicine (in the modern sense) are really in one way very like each other, because they are both very unlike the pure and abstract idea of Science as conceived by the Ancient Greeks. Science only means knowledge; and for those ancients it did only mean knowledge. They wanted nothing but the pleasure of knowing; they were particularly proud of knowing a great deal of utterly useless knowledge. Thus the favourite science of the Greeks was Astronomy, because it was as abstract as Algebra. And when the Philistine among them said: "What are the Pleiades to me?" the Philosopher really answered the Philistine by saying: "They are all the more to me because they are nothing to me." We may say that the great Greek ideal was to have no use for useful things. The Slave was he who learned useful things; the Freeman was he who learned useless things. This still remains the ideal of many noble men of science, in the sense that they do desire truth as the great Greeks desired it; and their attitude is an eternal protest against the vulgarity of utilitarianism. But there was and is another side of science, also to be respected, which was from the first represented by things like Medicine. And if there were some association of Medicine with Magic, it was because Magic was always extremely *practical*.

The modern Magician, often a most respectable gentleman, may have altered his opinion that sticking pins in the wax image of a politician would be a practical act of social utility. But so the modern Medicine-Man may have altered his opinion that the blood of badgers mixed with wine and salt is always an immediate cure for rheumatism. But there is nothing in this change of opinion on the mere fact or details that differs from any other modern change in medical method, as in curing consumption first by shutting all the windows and then by opening all the windows. The point is that both types of Medicine-Man were employed by people who wanted something prompt and practical, such as killing politicians or curing rheumatism. And the note of this sort of science, which Mr. Dawson traces to the East, is that it always boasts of possessing Power, as distinct from the other sort set upon enjoying Truth. We have most of us met the kind of theosophical mystic who is always whispering that he can show us the Path to Power; that if we will only say "I am Wisdom; I am Power", seventy-seven times before the looking-glass we shall control the cosmos. There was some such note even in mediæval medicine. Mediæval science was really more practical than Pagan science, but sometimes it did really sound a little too practical to be quite wholesome. So some modern hygienic idealists are rather more concerned about health than is quite healthy. It is hard to dwell perpetually on this element of power without poisoning it with some element of pride. So, queerly enough, Aladdin and his Wonderful Lamp really has some remote relation with the miracles of science, though hardly any with the miracles of religion.

THE present position of the Bright Young Thing, or Brilliant Young Cynic of a hard and realistic epoch, is so heartrendingly sad and pitiable that aged sentimentalists can only gaze at it through floods of senile tears. The cynics themselves, of course, do not believe in sentiment, but they embody a most poignant example of pathos. No orphan child, sprinkled with stage snow in a Victorian melodrama, was ever more obviously out in the cold; no Mariana in a moated grange, or highborn maiden in a palace tower, had ever so conspicuously got left.

The stages of the strange and tragic story are worthy of some sort of simple summary. To begin with, the modern cynic was in the position of a man whose father has quarrelled with his grandfather; and who is himself filled with a pious and filial yearning to quarrel with them both. The yearning is indeed pious in the sense of traditional, in so far as this family quarrel seems to be a tradition in the family. But for him the practical problem is the double problem of quarrelling with them both. And it is not easy to quarrel with them both. If in wandering about the moated grange or the ancestral garden, he is struck with horror at the sight of some feature recalling the peculiar tastes of his grandfather in his Classical or his Pre-Raphaelite period, he may perhaps break out into curses against his ancestor, and express his disagreement with his grandfather in the most disagreeable language he can command. And just as he is beginning to enjoy himself, he will realize with a shock that he is in the shameful and unnatural position of agreeing with his father. In a desperate attempt to balance this, he will fall back on the more natural and genial occupation of recalling in detail all the more repulsive vices and follies of his own father. And then he will realize abruptly that he is only repeating the catalogue of curses and crimes once uttered by the more quavering voice of his aged grandfather.

This curious tragi-comedy is always being re-enacted, especially in recent times, when any debate turns on philosophy as displayed in history. Thus, the young man who associated himself with the famous Pacifist vote at Oxford will, of course, affirm the ideal of Internationalism, and treat Nationalism as a prehistoric superstition handed down from anthropoid ages. He may often be heard saying that arms and armaments (two rather different things) are a relic of mediævalism, and that an internationalist of the twentieth century cannot be expected to go back to the Middle Ages. And then, perhaps, some friend of his who happens to

know something about history will point out to
him that going forward to Internationalism *is* going
back to the Middle Ages. For the very deep
chasms that now divide the different nations only
appeared like cracks when the mediæval system
broke up. It is absurd to class modern armaments
with mediæval armaments, for gunpowder even did
more to destroy the mediæval system than to preserve it. And the indignant intellectual cannot
make up his mind whether to admire gunpowder
because it was a scientific discovery or to deplore
gunpower because it is a patriotic weapon. He is
dizzy with the effort to keep at an equal distance
from his thirteenth-century grandfather and his
seventeenth-century father. We see a compact
case of this contradiction in the rather morbid talk
that may be heard here and there in connexion
with what is called "the next war." Oddly enough,
it is the same people who always teach us, in their
Outlines of History and Encyclopædias of Everything, that everything is always getting better and
better, and that even our most miserable contemporaries are more happy than their fathers—it is
these same people who always tell us that one slip
in modern diplomacy, or one falsehood in modern
journalism, may precipitate a towering and top-
pling horror of torture and panic far worse than
anything the world has ever known before. It
might well be asked, with a certain abstract
curiosity, why our civilization must produce the

very worst in the way of war, if it must produce the very best in the way of everything else.

I found another example of this strange parable of son, father, and grandfather in a book I happen to have read on a totally different subject. It is by Mr. Don Marquis, the eminent American writer, and contains many quaint and amusing ideas; though it rather tends to get into the rut of that sort of ridicule, by way of flippancies about Jehovah and Satan and saints and angels, which was rather funnier when it began in Voltaire than when it ended in Mark Twain. But what interests me about the book is this: that, while it resembles Mr. Shaw's *Black Girl in Search of God* in this sort of professional profanity, the writer is much more in earnest, and, therefore, much more lively and amusing, in emphasizing another idea, which has also been adumbrated by Mr. Shaw. I mean all that notion of Woman the Huntress, with terrified males fleeing before her nets and darts, or reluctant captives of her bow and spear. All of which is sup-posed to sound very modern, though in itself it is rather anti-feminist than anti-clerical. But I do not suppose it ever occurred to the anti-clerical author that this is exactly the attitude for which the world has reproached the more fanatical sort of clerics. It was precisely this "modern" view of Woman that really was expressed, and often exaggerated, by the first hermits fleeing into the desert, or the most fanatical monks only too near the borderline of the madness of the Manichees. To regard Woman wildly as an Unholy Terror, instead of rightly as a Holy Terror, was the abuse of asceticism; but it seems to have become quite useful and usual in modernity.

Here, again, the brilliant modern is bringing in as modernity something that was rather like one of the antics of antiquity; he is rushing back to his ascetical grandfather to escape from his romantic father. And the confusion in both cases is due to the same pathetic quality in his whole position. He is staggering about from century to century, because he has no real standing-ground of his own; and he has no standing-ground because he has destroyed anything on which he could stand. Modern youth has been blamed for bringing in a fashion of negro dances; but the one nigger antic I really regret is the dance which was once called "The Breakdown," which breaks down the dancing-floor and ends with the disappearance of the dancer and the dance. The objection to all this merely destructive thought is that eventually such destruction is self-destruction. The game of "breaking up the happy home," even when it is really a bright and breezy pastime, is necessarily a brief pastime; and in the end it is the players who come out of the ruins, houseless and homeless, to become broken men. That is why the first thing to be felt for them is a profound and genuine pity; a pity that is not in the least an ironic term for patronage. As we should be genuinely sorry for tramps and paupers who are materially homeless, so we should be sorry for those who are morally homeless, and who suffer a philosophical starvation as deadly as physical starvation. Not only is it true that some of the most modern philosophers are only trying to prove that we cannot have a philosophy; it is even more true that the most modern among the physical scientists are only trying to prove that science is not physical. It would be even truer to say that some of them are trying to prove that science is not science. For science is only an old word for knowledge; and knowledge is exactly what some of the new scientists say we can never obtain. All this, right or wrong, has left that generation in an unprecedented degree unprepared with any axioms on which to act, or any tests on which it could really rely. And it is especially awkward, when the young man who has never learned anything except how to hate his own father and grandfather, is suddenly called upon to love all men like brothers.

THERE was printed recently a very reasonable and well-poised criticism on the subject of Modern Poetry. Perhaps it took some examples of Modern Poetry a little more seriously than I can manage to do; for the Moderns, who talk about irresistible temptations to love, do not always realize that they themselves torture us with irresistible temptations to laughter. But, on the whole, the critic justified himself in preserving his gravity; keeping a straight face (as the Chinese would say) in the presence of some extracts of a gravity-removing nature. He did not merely despise the past; he justified the present by appeals to the past. His thesis was broadly this: that when the particular inspiration of a poetical period is exhausted, those who begin the next period are almost bound to begin it with very bare and even bald forms of expression. He based a plausible argument on the case of Wordsworth, pointing out that the poet's first attempts to find a more natural style appeared as a very naked style—or lack of style. If we accept the assumption that it was no longer possible for a man to write in the style of Dryden, even if "he had the mind," it is certainly true in that case that a more direct and unadorned manner appeared very crude and clumsy.

It did strike Wordworth's most cultured contemporaries as being not so much the appearance of a manner as the disappearance of manners. Wordsworth's new ballads were far less classical than the old ballads. Lines like "The more did his thick ankles swell" had not the natural dignity that belonged to most verses in "Chevy Chase" or "Sir Patrick Spens." It did seem like a change from natural dignity to natural indignity. And it is quite true, as the critic suggested, that this is very much the impression produced upon people of a more traditional culture by the ugliness of some modern verse. But it is perhaps an exaggeration to make Wordsworth a father and founder of the whole Romantic Movement, seeing that his friend Coleridge wrote a real old ballad in "The Ancient Mariner," with only one line "for which he was indebted to Mr. Wordsworth"; and seeing that Burns had already written and Byron was not far behind. And it marks something misleading in such sweeping classifications as "the Romantic School" that we have to class the jewelled casements of Keats with the blank and almost dead daylight of the first Lyrical Ballads. In short, the argument involves an ingenious suggestion, which in some aspects is really suggestive. But it is rather a gloomy and blasting prophecy to say that anybody who is to renew the life of English poetry must of necessity begin with writing such abominably bad poetry as some of the first poems of Wordsworth.

But another doubt stirred within me, after reading all such scientific analysis about the exhaustion of classic poetry in the eighteenth century, or of romantic poetry in the nineteenth century. My own early education, such as it was, dates from the very end of the nineteenth century; and it was a period in which people talked a great deal about religious doubt. Religious doubt produced a good deal of doubtful religion. We are now in a time when the world is more definitely divided into denials and affirmations, and is no longer merely enjoying its doubts. But I, for one, have found that one advantage of a man ceasing to doubt about religion is that he is much more free to doubt about everything else. All the nineteenth-century sceptics about the other world were dupes about this world. They accepted everything that was fashionable as if it were final; and the revolutionary romantics, who thought they would see the end of religion, never thought they would see the end of romance. Hence they encouraged this excessive habit of setting one style or school against another, and treated the victory of romanticism over classicism as the final victory of light over darkness. When there came in turn a victory of realism over romanticism, no people were more perplexed and irritated at the new revolution than the old revolutionists. Between them, it seems to me, they made far too much of all this grouping of literature under labels; and as they made too much of the label of Classical Poetry, and the label of Romantic Poetry, so they are now making far too much of the label of Modern Poetry.

What the world wants, what the world is waiting for, is not Modern Poetry or Classical Poetry or Neo-Classical Poetry—but Good Poetry. And the dreadful disreputable doubt, which stirs in my own sceptical mind, is a doubt about whether it would really matter much what style a poet chose to write in, in any period, so long as he wrote Good Poetry. Criticisms like that which I am criticizing always abound in phrases like "We can no longer use the romantic form," or "The atmosphere of the age forbids us to appeal to the eighteenth-century tradition," or "Modern poets, being forced to avoid the Pre-Raphaelite appeal," and so on. Now it is certainly true that we cannot write like Keats or Rossetti; at least I cannot, and it is just barely possible that you cannot. But the diabolical doubt still haunts me, about whether we would not if we could. Suppose a man were to produce, let us say, an imaginative fragment that was really as good as "Kubla Kahn," and more or less in the same diction as "Kubla Kahn"—is it really true that we should not admire it? Is it not even probable, on the whole, that he would admire it? Would he really say to himself: "Well, I have written these lines that seem haunting and resounding; I have created these images that seem magnetic and full of beckoning significance; I have composed something that would have made me as great as Coleridge, if I had lived in the time of Coleridge. But, of course, I shall instantly put it on the fire, because it is not obviously dated 1936–7. I should not dream of publishing it, because the atmosphere of the age forbids me to write good poetry in that particular manner. It is my duty to leave off, and begin to write bad poetry, in the hope that it may evolve into a real twentieth-century style"?

I am sorry, but the doubt still hagrides me about whether any human being would actually behave like that. Suppose somebody did write something that was melodious in the manner of "The Garden of Proserpine," or moving in the manner of "The Lake Isle of Innisfree," or even pictorial in the manner of "The Lady of Shalott," would he really drop all his dreams and be deaf to all his voices, for fear somebody should call him a Pre-Raphaelite? I have a dark and horrid suspicion that most modern poets have not resisted any such temptations, because they have not had any such inspirations. But if the inspirations were real inspirations of their kind, or of any kind, would anybody who loves poetry care a curse about whether the modern poets were being sufficiently modern?

Note that I am not saying for a moment that new writers must not try new styles. I am resisting the veto that they must not try old styles. I am questioning this incessantly repeated suggestion, that certain particular images or cadences or conceptions have become impossible to any literary man, because he has the misfortune to live at this particular moment by the clock. It seems to me to exaggerate our slavery to a season or a fashion, and to be a part of that sullen fatalism which may certainly be found in much modern poetry, but which is not poetical, but only modern. It is an irony that those who would most isolate art, in the manner that used to be called art for art's sake, are generally those who are most soaked and stagnantly drugged by the philosophy of their time. After all, "Lucy Gray" is not better than "Lycidas" even now; and I suspect some classic lines by Binyon or Belloc will last till they are no longer old. What about the new verses when they are no longer new?

PRESENTED in very large letters on the leader
page of a leading daily paper, I find the
statement that "the problem that besets the
most limpid of all America's blonde actresses . . .
is too many riches." Gazing at this announcement,
I fell into a trance of reflection, like those in which
many modern writers have seen visions of the
future. But I was only wondering in a vague way
what an average society, supposing it to be restored
to an average sanity, would really make of a sentence like that—if it were preserved like a papyrus
or a hieroglyphic in some museum of the future.
It is true, and our remote descendants might from
other sources have discovered it to be true, that
Americans in the nineteenth and even twentieth
century have had a curious passion for competitions.
Nothing is more popular as a topic in the trans-
atlantic Press than the action of somebody who
has been insane enough to select the Six Best Songs
or the Seven Best Sonnets or the Ten Best Tales of
True Romance. In some moral matters Americans
have a real enthusiasm for equality; and their
democratic instincts are very deep and will not
easily be uprooted, even in these undemocratic

days. But in other intellectual matters, perhaps because they really care less about intellectual matters, they may be said to have a passion for inequality. That is, they have a passion for classification; and they treat it as a sort of prodigiously and portentously solemn sport. Some complain that their sport is not sporting. I would not go so far; but I think it is even truer of them than of us that their sport is not sportive. Therefore they enter with excitement upon these scientific sports, which are supposed to deal with statistics and averages, but draw their inner life from an intense love of comparison and competition. All these scientific judgments are really modelled on the simple artistic judgment, which I once heard from a most charming American amid the landscape of the Alps: "Well, I can't see, when you've seen the highest mountain in Switzerland, what you want to see any more for." In his view the various Alpine peaks had run a sort of race, and the peak that reached the highest point was superior in that and every other respect. When we really understand that, we can sympathize with pie-eating contests or men sitting for weeks on end in a tree—or even with less intelligent enterprises, like committees for Eugenic legislation or Intelligence Tests designed to discover whether immigrants from the countries of Dante or Copernicus are or are not human beings.

So far all is clear; or shall we say limpid? This

appetite for competition and comparison is a national characteristic like any other; sometimes inspiriting, sometimes amusing; we can sympathize with it, and our posterity might in some degree sympathize with it. So long as it measures the height of foreign mountains or the contour of foreigners' skulls, it is at least measuring things that are measurable. And there is a good deal of innocent fun in it, even when it is applied where it is obviously inapplicable; to measure things that are in their nature immeasurable. It might be quite amusing to capture every wandering Pegasus, ridden by every lonely poet, and organize them all with weights and handicaps as a horse-race. It might be entertaining to record that the sea-shanty of The Drunken Sailor has closed in a dead heat with the *Dies Iræ,* or that "Sally in Our Alley" has beaten "I'll Sing Thee Songs of Araby" by a length and a half. I have no very clear idea what it means, but those who organize it certainly mean no harm. Also, to do them justice, they are generally thinking about things that are to some extent practical and real; such as popularity or power of emotional effectiveness on particular occasions; sometimes, I fear, they are thinking about things still more practical, such as money. Up to a point, I am willing to be excited when they discuss what is the most popular song or the most beautiful woman; though I never saw the picture of a prizewinner in any Beauty Competition without thinking that I knew several better-looking women living in my own street. I should therefore accept, with a slight sigh, the statement that somebody was the most beautiful of all America's blonde actresses. But surely it is by some more curious convolutions of thought that anybody can reach so firm and fixed a belief that she is "the most limpid of all America's blonde actresses."

It seems to be assumed that all America's blonde actresses are engaged in a fierce competition for limpidity—whatever that may be. Not without bitter rivalries and breathless jealousies has the peculiar palm been won. Challenges have been issued to the multitudinous towns and villages of the vast prairies and the wide, open spaces where blondes are blondes. Indignant families have declared that our Sadie is as limpid as any of these dames down east; and Clytie has told her sisters that she means to be just as limpid as she knows how. The cry of "Limpid is my middle name" has resounded from the Atlantic to the Pacific, and numberless aspirants have assured themselves that they are just too limpid to live—before this tremendous trial of strength was decided. Possibly its echoes may have been heard even in foreign lands, and inspired the blondes of other races; except, I presume, the negro race, among whom blondes are said to be comparatively rare. The French soldier, sinking to repose to the charming tune of "Auprès de ma blonde qui fait bon dormi," may rouse himself with a start of suspicion and hiss the fatal question: "But is she limpid?" The German Hitlerite, now prostrate in worship of the Blonde Beast, which is his version of the Blonde Beauty, may wonder for a moment whether it is wholly, utterly, and completely limpid; which, to judge by the new German ideals as explained in the old German literary style, it is not. But in that respect the most obscure German diction is not much more bewildering than our own journalistic diction. What are we to say about that indescribable sort of newspaper writing to be noted in the example I have given? What in the world does all this sort of thing mean; and what are the vague and vast implications behind it? Why is the writer so frightfully certain that the lady is the most limpid of all American blondes, and what precisely does he mean by the epithet? The present age may be producing the most limpid blondes, but hardly the most limpid writers.

The truth is that the sort of journalism which now specially professes to be fresh, up to date, on the spot, and as new as the latest news, is, in a very peculiar sense, a residuum of stale things out of the past; an accumulation of antiquated associations of which the very origin is lost, and more like the end of everything than the beginning of anything. It is always using terms that have grown colourless through oblivion of their original context, which are now used rather with a hazy appreciation of their sound than a logical appreciation of their sense. I have called it indescribable; and it is really very difficult to describe. It goes far beyond what was once condemned as journalese, in the sense of being jaunty and even vulgar. It is a sort of jargon drawn from all sorts of languages, some of them æsthetic or scientific in origin; all these scraps of culture are now loose in the world; but, though everything is loose, nothing is lost, except the tradition of how to treat them reasonably. We have turned scientific language into a sort of slang; the sort of slang that is used to save trouble. Anybody can talk about problems and nobody need bother about solutions; anybody is free to talk about a complex so long as he can ignore its complexity; anybody can borrow a word from the studios or the workshops, so long as he does not pay it back by making any study or doing any work.

Some people seem ready to call this limpid; but I should be inclined to call it limp. The increasing inconclusiveness of most articles in the Press and elsewhere seems to me the most disquieting mark of our mental development. It is not found only in sentimental and sensational headlines, such as that I have quoted; indeed, the end of such an article is even more limp than the beginning. We may yet live to regret the passing of the political party slanging-match or the mere newspaper sensation. They were at least limpid.

At this time many are writing about Coleridge; and there is no writer about whom
it is so difficult to write. Coleridge was a remark-
able man in many departments, about which
writing would not be so difficult; the difficulty is in
dealing with the department in which he did
certain things, a very few things, that make it
essential to write about him at all. He was and he
achieved many things that could be criticized with
some fruitfulness and profit. He was a transcen-
dental theorist who came to be of some importance
as a theologian; and he is the fountain of some very
fine thinking among the liberal theologians of the
old school, like Maurice and Robertson. He was a
figure of some political and historical interest, since
he began with an enthusiasm for the French
Revolution and ended with an enthusiasm for the
German metaphysics; and, of the two great
catastrophes, I personally prefer the first. He
was a great Character; one of those men of whom
numberless anecdotes are told, chiefly to the effect
that his conversation was fascinating and continuous; some found it too fascinating; some even
found it too continuous. There is the famous
story of the man whom Coleridge buttonholed in
the street and proceeded to talk to about Plato at

some length; whereupon the man, having an appointment, delicately and tactfully cut off the button and went about his business. Returning later by the same street, he saw Coleridge still holding the button and still talking about Plato. He wrote a number of minor works, generally dismissed in the discussion of his genius, which are decidedly clever and ought not to be dismissed so easily. For instance, in the days of his French Revolutionary enthusiasm, he wrote a satiric poem against Pitt, which I still think very fine; but partly perhaps because I am all in favour of people writing satiric poems against Pitt. This poem, as everybody knows, is a masque of Fire, Famine and Slaughter; in which these plagues of mankind attribute their power to Pitt, but two of them eventually turn upon him. Fire, however, amiably observes:

> I alone am faithful; I
> Cling to him everlastingly.

There is no liberal theology about that.

I repeat, therefore, that there are many things about him that could be profitably criticized. Unfortunately, there are one or two things that cannot be criticized. They can only be quoted. Nor have I any intention of filling up the blanks of this essay by quoting them. But the point about Coleridge is that the peaks of his imagination, though few and rare, are absolutely above criticism.

They live by that mysterious life of the imagination, which is something much more terrible than an anarchy. For it has laws of its own which man has never been able to turn into a code. But anybody who understands poetry knows when poetry has fulfilled those laws; as certainly as a mathematician knows when a mathematical calculation is correct. Only, the mathematician can explain, more or less, why the answer is exactly right; and the lover of poetry can never explain why the word or the image is exactly right. It is obvious, on the face of it, that "Kubla Khan" is a piece of pure nonsense. There is no earthly connexion— we might perhaps accentuate the phrase no *earthly* connexion—between the architectural tastes of Kubla and the misfortunes of a lady who was wailing for her demon lover; and still less connexion between this tragedy and the rejoicings round a gentleman who on honey-dew had fed and drunk the milk of paradise. Yet any mind moving by the laws of the imagination knows that all these three things are one thing, and the poem is one poem. The poet is riding the air on the imagination alone; and his Pegasus has wings and no feet. But almost all that has been attempted, in the way of analysing those imaginative laws, has been done by some metaphysician, who has feet and no wings.

It seems to me that the central genius of a man like Coleridge is not a thing to be dealt with by critics at all. If they really had anything worth saying about such a poet, they would write it in poetry. It is the curse upon all critics that they must write in prose. It is the specially blighting and blasting curse upon some of them, that they have to write in philosophical or psychological or generally analytical prose. I have never read a page of such criticism, however clear and clever, which brought me the most remote echo of the actual sound of the poetry or the power of poetical images, which are like magic talismans. Therefore, in writing about a man like Coleridge, we are driven back upon secondary things; upon his second best work, or upon the second- or third-rate controversies aroused by that work. In that sense, of course, there are any number of second-rate things to be said of Coleridge. It is suggested, for instance, that the abnormal or enormous enlargement of his imagination was due to a dirty habit he had of taking opium. I will confess that I am sceptical about the divinity of the drug; or the power of any drug to act like a god, and make a man other than he really is. I will merely suggest that if exactly the same quantity of opium had been given to a number of Coleridge's contemporaries—let us say to George the Third, to Mr. Bentham, to the Duke of Wellington, to Mr. Gifford, to Beau Brummel or to William Pitt himself, not to mention Mr. Perceval—I gravely doubt whether any or all of these persons together would have produced a line of "Kubla Khan." It was a pity that Coleridge took opium; because it dissolved his great intellect in dreams, when he was perhaps more fitted than most men of his time to have made some structural logical system, that should have reconciled Revolution and Religion. But "Christabel" and "The Ancient Mariner" were written by Mr. Coleridge and not by Mr. Opium. The drug may have accelerated or made easy a work which some weaknesses in his moral character might have made him avoid or delay, because they were laborious; but there is nothing creative about a narcotic. The point is perhaps worthy of remark; for nobody who knows the nineteenth-century literature can fail to notice that there was a curious effort, under the surface, to make such Asiatic drugs as normal as European drinks. It is a sort of subterranean conspiracy that ranges from the *Confessions* of De Quincey to the *Moonstone* of Wilkie Collins. Fortunately, tradition was too strong for it; and Christian men continued to prefer the grape of life to the poppy of death.

Then it would be easy to add, upon this secondary plane, that Coleridge did really suffer from other misleading influences besides opium. "The Ancient Mariner" is probably one of the most original poems that were ever written; and, like many original things, it is almost antiquarian. Like most Romantics reviving the Gothic without understanding the mediæval, he carried archaism

to lengths that were almost comic. I am not sure
that he did not call the Mariner a Marinere. All
that affects us as too reminiscent of the Olde
English Tea-Shoppe. A more serious difficulty was
that he turned too sharply from France to Germany.
It was very natural that a Romantic should take
refuge in the German forests, and still more in the
German fairy-tales. It was a more unfortunate
adventure that he took refuge with the German
philosophers. They encouraged him, as did the
drug, in a sort of misty infinity, which confused his
real genius for definition and deduction. It was in
every way excellent, of course, that the great
German literature of the great German age, the
age of Goethe and of Lessing, should be opened
up to English readers; and perhaps it could have
been done by Coleridge more calmly and luminously
than it was afterwards done by Carlyle. But if
Goethe was the great and good influence of Germany, Kant was on the whole the great and bad
influence. These two great Germans offer any
number of aspects to be admired or criticized; but,
on the whole, Goethe made Germany a part of
Europe, while Kant cut it off from Europe, following a wild light of its own, heaven knows where.
Coleridge the philosopher can be criticized on various grounds; including the ground that he did not
know the great philosopher of Christendom that was
behind him. But Coleridge the poet cannot be criticized at all.

NEW movements in literature are those which copy the last century but one. If they copy the last century, they are old-fashioned; but if it is quite clear that they are much more than a hundred years old, they are entirely fresh and original. It is true that there are certain literary men, claiming to inaugurate literary movements, who try to avoid the difficulty by various methods; as by writing their poetry upside down, or using words that consist entirely of consonants; or publishing a book of entirely blank pages, with a few asterisks in the middle to show that there is a break in the narrative. These or similar scribes are conjectured to be trying to copy the literature of the next century. They may freely be left for that century—to forget. Moreover, parallel perversities, if not exactly the same ones, are also to be found scattered through the centuries of the past. Of such a kind, for instance, were the Renaissance games or sports which consisted of shortening or lengthening the lines of poetry, so as to make the whole poem a particular shape, such as the shape of a heart or a cross or an eagle. Anyhow, if we eliminate a few such eccentric experimentalists, who think they anticipate the intelligence of the future by being unintelligible in the present, the general rule about change and rejuvenation in literature is much as I have stated it. It is essential for the pioneer and prophet, not so much to go forward very far, as to go back far enough. The general rule is to skip a century, as some hereditary features are said to skip a generation. There is something very odd about this system of alternation, black and white like a chessboard. It is as if every man always hated his father and adored his grandfather.

About some epochs of culture, all this is fairly well known and fairly widely admitted. Most people realize, for instance, that the Romantics of the nineteenth century were appealing back to the more purely poetical poets of the seventeenth century, against the almost prosaic poets of the eighteenth. Indeed, Romanticism, though it so often went with Revolutionism, was in its very nature a more general appeal to the past. Perhaps the most genuinely and practically effective popularizer of the new Romanticism was Sir Walter Scott, whose truest title is The Antiquary. But the same is true, of course, of the other Romantics who were not, as Scott was, personally Tory and traditional. Coleridge's "Ancient Mariner" was taken as the very type of a new and original and even fantastic form in literature. Yet the "Ancient Mariner" has a form, and it happens to be an entirely antiquated form. The Ancient Mariner was a very Ancient Mariner. Even Byron was always looking backward, and he died not for the modern Liberals, but for the ancient Greeks. Had he been a true Progressive, and observed the gradual improvement in all things, by the substitution of higher for lower civilization, he would, of course, have preferred to reverence the more recent phenomenon of the Turks. But, generally speaking, it is true to say that the modern Romantics were not really looking to the sunrise; they were pursuing a most gorgeous and glorious sunset, of which the last trail and after-glow vanished with Crashaw and the Cavalier mystics. The men of the nineteenth century were following the men of the seventeenth century; the last century but one. Anyhow, the last century is the last century men will follow.

What is not so clearly seen is that the same is true of the twentieth century; and the twentieth century also is copying the last century but one. In short, it is copying the eighteenth century, and especially all that was most hated and condemned in the work of the eighteenth century. This is specially true of two outstanding features which many have thought to be a great deal too outstanding. They specially imitate, among the elements of the eighteenth century, its coarseness and its coldness. I do not necessarily use these terms merely as terms of abuse; it is much more

important that the new writers themselves will use
them as terms of praise. They would describe
the coarseness as candour and the coldness as
detachment; and in this again the eighteenth and
the twentieth centuries would meet. But we get no
farther in such a matter by selecting terms of
praise or blame for an objective fact of history. A
young writer to-day does not admit that he is less
educated because he uses the words which old
writers learned in the gutter and the greasy tavern.
He does not admit that he is less humanistic because his characters behave in as inhuman a manner
as the tricky and treacherous and heartless lovers in
the old cynical comedies.

These new writers are making a new attempt to
find civilization along the old rationalistic road,
which is now nearly two hundred years old, rather
than along the romantic road, which is only a
hundred. Allowing for the inevitable but incidental difference in the details of the day, which
have to be discussed, the spirit of the Very Modern
Young Man is the spirit of a man in a three-
cornered hat and a powdered wig. Much as may
be said about disorder in the arts, there is another
side to the recent realism of literature. It has its
own kind of neatness, just as it has its own kind
of nastiness. The same can be said of the detailed
drawings of Hogarth. Even its extravagances are
more often satires and less often visions. Mr.
Aldous Huxley much more clearly suggests a

return to Swift than an extension of Yeats. Mr. Yeats will not care about that, partly because he is too great a man to care, and partly because nobody has a finer admiration for Swift than he. But obviously the ruthlessness of *Brave New World* is more like the ruthlessness of *Gulliver's Travels* than it is like the more optimistic ruthlessness of the nineteenth-century visits to Utopia or the Earthly Paradise, in books like *News from Nowhere* or *New Worlds for Old*. It is equally obvious, in the debates about sex, that men like Mr. Aldous Huxley, following on men like Mr. Bernard Shaw, have been merely rebelling against that Romance which was itself a rebellion; rebellion against the realism and common sense of the age of rapiers and snuff-boxes. Much that is called immoral in a modern novel might have been called highly moral in an eighteenth-century tract, warning the young of the close connexion between the girls and the gallows. Sentimentalism is a mere catchword; but, anyhow, we do not entirely solve the puzzle we call Progress by looking at the pictures of The Rake's Progress or The Harlot's Progress. Those who despise sentimentalism now have rather a tendency to talk as if nobody had ever despised sentimentalism before. And so the rather feverish youthful genius in Chelsea or Bloomsbury feels that he alone has flung off all the fetters of all the ages when he braces himself with a bold effort to say something daring and destructive and then says exactly what Dr. Johnson would have said.

Nobody supposes such parallels are complete. Nobody supposes that such comparisons are concerned with mere copies. It does not follow that the new writer has not something in him that is really new; or, what is much more important, something that is really his own. The point is that such inspiration as he does invoke does not come from the newer things, but rather from the older things. The poets of the Sitwell family, for instance, have been both chaffed and flattered for introducing newer things; but, in fact, they are particularly fond of the older things. Their taste in gimcracks is exactly the eighteenth-century taste; when one of them gives Apollo a "golden peruke," we see a hundred embroidered pictures or painted tiles in old mansions and museums; and Miss Edith Sitwell has written what would be the best, if it were not the only, sustained eulogy on Pope.

I HAPPENED to meet again, recently, after many
years, a very brilliant and distinguished Italian
professor who specializes in the study of English
literature. And almost the first words he spoke to
me, with more than Italian vivacity and even
agitation, were: "What has happened to George
Meredith?"

He said it as if George Meredith were still alive,
but had been missing for three days from his Surrey
home; as if fears were entertained that he might
have fallen off Box Hill or been battered featureless
by the traffic in Guildford High Street; as if all
England were searching for the missing novelist and
Scotland Yard was believed to be in possession of
a clue. But I knew my Italian friend's meaning
much better. What puzzled him was not that all
England was searching for George Meredith, but
rather that all England was not searching for
George Meredith; or even searching for George
Meredith's books. And it gave me an increased
respect for the acumen and vigilance with which
he followed our island literature, to know that he
had noticed this very curious blank and even
oblivion that has followed on so much admitted

brilliance and fame. To any one who remembers, as I do, the days when Meredith was not merely the idol of the intellectuals, but regarded by all the intelligent as one out of the two or three really great men who could be regarded as leaders of the literature of England in the face of Europe, there is something very extraordinary about this capricious and sudden silence. It is all the more extraordinary because of the ideas for which Meredith stood and the qualities which his admirers chiefly admired. It seemed to most of us, in our boyhood, that he was not only the greatest literary artist then present, but that he was prophetically the first literary artist of the future. He was not only the greatest English author alive, but the only English author who would live. And yet he has not really lived; certainly he has not yet really triumphed. He was the champion of all the things that were expected to triumph; nay, the things that many people tell us have already triumphed. He was, for instance, the champion of Feminism. I do not say that his "Ballad of Fair Ladies in Revolt" could actually have been sung as a marching song by the well-drilled battalions of Mrs. Pankhurst. For Meredith's literary style did not always lend itself to being used as a roaring chorus for the march or the camp-fire. But, in its philosophy, it expressed almost everything that the Suffragettes wanted to say, and was, in form, more philosophical and intellectual than most of the things they did say. He anticipated the re-action against the Rhodes and Rudyard Kipling type of Imperialism, and urged the sympathetic comprehension of the Celt against the more arro-gant nineteenth-century nonsense about the uni-versal superiority of the Anglo-Saxon. True, he was enough of a nineteenth-century man to trace these differences almost entirely along the lines of race, and to be entirely ignorant, for instance, of the extent to which they followed the lines of religion. But that was not so much because he had the limitations of a nineteenth-century man as because he had the even narrower limitations of a free-thinker.

Anyhow, in a score of ways, the modern world has followed the Meredithean model for the world, and one could have sworn that he was safe for a much frequented shrine in the Pantheon of Prog-ress. A much more frequented shrine, in fact, is that of Thomas Hardy, who was also a free-thinker, but a much less practical friend to freedom. Hardy was, indeed, full of the sense of numberless things that ought to be done, but it was somewhat softened and mellowed by a persistent doubt about whether they could be done. But Meredith was the sort of nineteenth-century Liberal who was full of a flaming certainty that they would be done; and they were done. But he has no particular credit now for having helped to do them. And it seems, in some strange sense, that it is Meredith himself

who is done. I would not disgrace my own older
generation by saying for a moment that he is done
for, but there seem to be large numbers of the
newer generation who act on the assumption that
he is done with.

I am well aware, of course, that these political
and sociological aspects are quite secondary in the
estimate of a great master of imaginative fiction;
a man who could create men, and especially women.
But such things as his failure to figure, even as a
memory, in what many would call the victory of
women really is part of a whole comparison that is
something of a puzzle. Nothing was more puzzling,
for instance, than the strange story of the two
funerals, the funeral of Meredith and the funeral
of Hardy. Enthusiasts, if I remember rightly, demanded a grave for Meredith in Westminster
Abbey; and it was refused. Enthusiasts demanded
a grave for Hardy in Westminster Abbey; and it
was at least partially, or by some compromise,
granted. I cannot imagine why. If it were a question of literary fame, Meredith stood then even
higher than Hardy. If it were a question of incon-
gruity of religion or irreligion, the objection was
infinitely stronger against Hardy than against
Meredith. Hardy, with all his virtues, or possibly
as one of his virtues, was quite frankly provocative atheist and pessimist. Meredith was not a
provocative atheist and not a pessimist at all. A
man might read five volumes of Meredith and not

find a single direct taunt like that about the President of the Immortals delighting in the torture of Tess.

It was not so much that Meredith did not worship God as that he did worship Nature. And perhaps that is where the breach has come between him and the new sceptics, who are often more bitterly at war with Nature than with God. There are even hints in the work of later sceptics, like Mr. Aldous Huxley and others, that, if they were absolutely driven to the alternative, they would rather take refuge with the supernatural than with the natural. Perhaps Meredith inherited even too much of that sentiment, which was spread all over that century, from Wordsworth to Whitman, that the earth is itself a healer and all its green and growing things are a hope. Yet Meredith was sound and sincere in his own particular version of this vision—that of the wilderness as a sort of garden of medicinal herbs; nor is he proved wrong by the mere fact of another generation of the young, with quite exceptionally sour stomachs, thinking that the physic is nasty. But even if this be granted as a fair difference of opinion, it does not explain the decline of interest in all that once made Meredith most interesting. It does not explain the lack of memory or allusion concerning the real business of the novelist as a novelist. His character drawing surely remains unquestionably lively and sympathetic. Moreover, though he delighted in a sort of sophistication, it is by no means true that he only wrote about the sophisticated. Following the sad habit of the times, it is long since I have read the greater part of Meredith; but I think the thing that stands out with most startling veracity in my memory is his description of ordinary schoolboys. I shall never forget the moment when some boy—Harry Richmond, I think—is challenged by another boy to repeat the word "fool," and then to repeat it twenty times. And, "with a seriousness of which only boys and such barbarians are capable," Harry actually recited the word with precisely the required number of repetitions. There is nothing perverse or euphuistic about that; and we are always certain, in Meredith's books at least, that boys will be boys. The truth is that Meredith was both full-blooded and also foppish and even foolish. He was affected because he was vain, but he was vain because he was natural. We might understand him better as an artist of the Renaissance.

As I am myself a Liberal without any Liberal
Party; a Little-Englander in the sense that I
care more about England than about Newfound-
land or Tasmania; a Radical in all my instincts in
the general social quarrels of our plutocracy; an
ex-Socialist who is still enough of a Socialist to be
a sort of revolutionist, and to regret that the
Socialists have become as respectable as the Prime
Minister; a Distributist who denies that any of the
nineteenth-century parties of squires and merchants had the remotest notion of what was wrong
with the nineteenth century, especially in England
(for what was wrong was the absence of peasants,
who are equally opposed to merchants and squires)
—in short, since I am a disreputable demagogic
sort of person, holding that most reforms are too
slow rather than too fast—from all this it will be
easily and naturally deduced that my favourite
politician is Mr. Baldwin. The deduction may not
be swift and obvious; but it is sound. When I say
my favourite politician, I mean in so far as any
politician can be anybody's favourite. I do not take
the taste with tremendous solemnity; because our
politicians do not control our politics. Even the best
of them are forced to a continuous compromise
by the pressure of private interests, which are also
public monopolies; and it is these commercial

monopolies that rule the State. But if I were in practical politics (which God forbid), and if they involved me in that particular problem of party allegiance, I should support Mr. Baldwin for all I was worth, or rather for all he is worth—which is not a little. I should support him even though I disagree with him; on the ground that at least he is more liberal than the Liberals, more social than the Socialists, and immeasurably more patriotic than the Imperialists. I should support him through thick and thin; for I think the opposing theories are pretty thin and the impudence a bit thick. I should support him especially against his loyal and devoted followers.

But I value him very specially for this: that I do think he is the one politician alive who has some inner understanding of the English people. They are exceedingly difficult to understand. So far from being merely bluff and sturdy, as they used to imagine, they are by far the most subtle and complex of all the great nations of Christendom. Since the fall of the Stuarts, with the beginning of the eighteenth century, their system has worked with a quite abnormal sort of anonymity and evasiveness. At that date they set up a king who was not allowed to govern anything and an aristocracy which in reality governed everything, but which went on saying louder and louder that it governed nothing and was not an aristocracy at all. All our chief official figures are unofficial; they are in that sense outsiders. The Prime Minister is an outsider, for he is unknown to the British Constitution. The Speaker is so called because he is the one Member who never speaks. The Cabinet carries with it the suggestion of a secret meeting; or men hiding in a corner, or even locked up in a box. For the only lawful power was in the Privy Council, which never meets at all. The power has passed to something much privier than a Privy Council. These are only instances taken at random; these and a thousand other things illustrate the strange quality I have mentioned; the quality of evasiveness; we might say of escape. And the most singular form of it is that to which I have already referred, the curious anonymity of aristocracy. For two centuries, and at least up to very lately, England has been a State of a special historical type. It was a type very common in mercantile and seafaring States; as in the Republic of Venice and the Republic of Holland. One feature of these Republics was that they were not republican— in the modern sense of democratic. But the feature of England was more odd and unique. It was, in effect, that aristocrats could do anything except call themselves aristocrats. They must be very careful only to call themselves gentlemen. It may seem a very vague and irrational understanding, but upon that understanding rested the safety of a vast and often victorious system; and, for some time at least, the greatness of England.

Now when the quarrel began about the Blackshirts and the Red Peril in England, Mr. Baldwin said one very profound and penetrating thing. Nobody else said it; and nobody seems to have taken any particular notice of it. What he said was, in substance, this, or words to the same effect. Whatever you may think about rival theories or systems, the fact will remain that Communists generally are poor men and Fascists generally are not. He was right; and it is unfortunately the fact, in England, that a fight between them will seem to be simply a fight of rich men as such against poor men as such. And *that* is precisely the one thing that the policy of a popular gentry must avoid as a matter of life and death. Cynically speaking, it may have any amount of general injustice, in the impersonal pressure of one economic class upon another. But if you can actually take a snapshot of the squire kicking the poacher, if you can prove the practical occurrence of a banker bashing a beggar on the head—then you explode the whole generous fiction on which the popularity of a gentry reposes. Anybody who does not understand that does not understand the English people; and Mr. Baldwin does.

It is not so with the same factions of Fascists and Communists on the Continent. For on the Continent the traditions of a conflict of ideas have come down continuously from the Crusades and the religious wars and the wars of the French Revolution. And the intellectual vision, even the enemy's intellectual vision, is often vivid enough to make men forget the mere facts of wealth and poverty. When a Crusader fought with a Saracen, it might happen that the Crusader was a poor knight or squire driven to the wars by sheer poverty and the other a great Sheik with whole processions of camels and concubines. Or it might equally happen that the Crusader was a rich and powerful baron and the Moslem a poor and ragged Bedouin. But it was in the whole temper of the time to think of it first as a fight between Christendom and Islam. So, even in England, as late as the genuine struggle of Roundheads and Cavaliers, the Cavalier might be a great noble like Newcastle, or he might be a nameless yeoman from loyal Hereford or Cornwall. The Roundhead might be a tinker like Bunyan, though he was quite as likely to be a Puritan aristocrat rich with the abbey lands, or a wealthy London merchant. But there remained some true feeling that it was the anointed King against the Parliament— or the Saints. So in Europe still, whatever be the facts, it is felt as a fight between a Fascist who does believe in the Corporative State and a Communist who does believe in the Communist State. But, for good or evil, we have never got ideas worked into the popular intelligence, as on the Continent. We have forgotten the fight about ethics, and are left with the depressing substitute of economics. With us it would really be a Class War; but with them it is only the last of the Wars of Religion.

NOBODY seems to have seen, in the current tendency to express party politics by means of Shirts,
a new opportunity for expressing them in the
shades of Shirts. Hitherto colours have been used
heraldically, in the manner of people blazoning
or brandishing flags; and not æsthetically, in the
manner of people choosing or matching neckties.
Yet it would seem an excellent opportunity for a
thoughtful citizen to suggest the idea that he is
Rather Nazi or Not Quite Communist. A wise and
well-balanced Hitlerite, if such a monster is allowed
to survive, might express his doubts by having his
new brown shirt fade faintly into the old field-grey,
or having it shot with the richer colour of the
Red International. An Irishman disposed towards
compromise (if such a creature be among the
varieties of nature) might very well gratify General
O'Duffy by wearing a blue shirt, but introduce into
it a tint of peacock-blue, verging upon peacock-
green, to indicate his essentially unbroken loyalty
to the more normal national badge and to the
Wearing of the Green. I fear it is only too true
that a great many people now calling themselves
Socialists ought to be dressed not in red, but in

pink. And though I am no admirer of Bolshevism, I am still less of an admirer of pink. Pink seems to me the essentially false and negative colour; because it is the dilution of something that is rich and glowing or nothing. I do not object to pale blue, because it is sky-blue, and I graciously grant permission to the University of Cambridge to continue to employ the emblem of its traditional tint. But the sky is in its nature pale and translucent; it is the vehicle of light; it is sometimes actually white and blank; and the infusion of a faint and rather cold colour like blue is appropriate to it. But pink suggests nothing but the horrible and blasphemous idea of wine with too much water in it. Pink is the withering of the rose and the fading of the fire; pink is mere anæmia in the blood of the universe. And there is a merely pink humanitarianism which I dislike even more than the real Red Communism. It is not so honest; it is not so genuinely angry or so justly angry; and it is ultimately every bit as negative and destructive of the strong colours and definite shapes of any great historical culture. It will not weaken civilization the less because it is too watery to burn it in a night; for you cannot set fire to a town with pink torches or pink artillery. This cold and colourless sentimentalism none the less threatens the world like a slow and crawling Deluge. It especially threatens the colours of the world. It is a wash-out.

With this melancholy exception of the pink

social reformers, however, it is curious to notice
that the difference of shirts, with its opportunity
for the difference of shades, has appeared at the
very moment when such fine shades are most
furiously and impatiently disregarded. The old
rosettes of Buff and Blue were all cut to one pattern
and coloured with one dye; as if to make it impossible for men to express personality in party politics
or to effect compromise in party divisions. There
was no green in the Orangeman's eye, or in the fine
shades of the Tory True Blue. And yet, in the
actual centre of our parliamentary politics, the
colours ran into each other much more easily than
the vivid patches of the patchwork Europe of
to-day. Men were solemnly brought up as Whigs
and Tories; but there was much less difference
between the Whig and the Tory than there is to-day
between a Fascist who has been a Syndicalist and
a Communist who has been an Anarchist. Our
rigid party system did not need to stretch; because
the two parties were already stationed in close
proximity. An older analogy than the comparison
of flags and shirts, of uniforms and underclothing,
can be found in the more or less unique architectural structure of the English House of Com-
mons. I do not refer to what is, perhaps, the most
English thing about it; that it is actually built on
the assumption that a large number of its members
will never turn up. I mean that we have again the
paradox that there is most apparent division of

parties exactly where there is least real division of principles. The Continental Parliaments are nearly all of them arranged on the principle of a Curve of Relativity; almost like that of Einstein. The seats are arranged in a crescent only tending to two extremes at its two horns; the positions known as the Extreme Right and the Extreme Left. But any number of people can sit left of the Right and right of the Left. And I believe these intermediate seats are or were chosen in a more or less symbolic manner, to show that a member is more Radical than one group, but less Radical than another; as a man might say he was more Socialist than Mr. Lansbury but less Socialist than Mr. Maxton. For nobody could possibly be less Socialist than Mr. Mac-Donald.

This method of relative Left and Right really is the sort of thing that bears some resemblance to a Communist having a red shirt and a Socialist a pink shirt. That is, it allows of degree and fine shades of individuality. On the other hand, the very shape of the British Houses of Parliament seems designed for the most drastic party discipline and the most unwavering party choice. There are only two sides in the parliamentary chamber; as there were primarily only two sides in the parliamentary system. They face each other stiffly, like two lines deployed in battle; yet, as a matter of fact, there has been very much less battle. It was in the Continental council chambers, curved to

follow every gradation of thought and allowing for all compromises between all extremes,
that desks have been most frequently broken,
ink-bottles most vigorously hurled, riots most frequently prolonged into the night, and duels most
eagerly appointed for the morning.

I think this worth noting just now, because it
confirms something I said recently about a real
fallacy in the particular fashion now seeking to
improve upon Parliament. I hope nobody will
accuse me of the fatuous official optimism which
still talks as if Parliament could not be improved.
Whatever else we may think of the practical
architecture of St. Stephen's chamber, I trust no
sane people differ about the vastness and vista of
the room for improvement. Indeed, one of the
very worst things about Parliament is the parliamentary defence of Parliament. Politicians are
using the same silly tricks of smug secrecy and
evasion, which they used over the most trivial
intrigues in the institution, as a belated and blundering defence of the institution itself. They
have never had any notion of defending a thing,
except proving it to be indefensible by leaving it
undefended. They say nothing about the real
distrust now so widely felt, when financial corrup-
tion has been followed by financial collapse. But
there is something to be said for Parliament; at
least there is something to be said against the
Fascists who would merely destroy Parliament.

And it is expressed in the paradox that the very
mildest of all party systems was expressed in the
military regimentation of its benches or the heraldic
fixity of its badges. Foreigners had fights, which
were not designed and occurred from time to time.
We had a sham fight, which was designed, and
which occurred all the time. But behind that sham
fight was much more of unity; possibly far too
much unity. Therefore the Totalitarian State, with
its one badge, its one bench and its one party, is
not a cure for the old evils of the English party
system. It was much too Totalitarian a State already.
Its apparent party divisions were merely a popular
sport, like the Boat Race; which is also the one
and only example I know of shirts, ties, and badges
being differentiated only by two shades of the same
colour.

A TREMENDOUS international truth dawned upon
me the other day in connexion with the subject of dress clothes, which we rather incorrectly
call evening dress. For in that shade of difference there is a deep and strange division, and
a sort of abyss yawns between England and Europe. The occasion of the thought may appear
somewhat trivial for so vast and solemn a matter.
I met an educated and experienced Englishman,
in a great Italian city in which he had apparently
lived for about fifteen years. But the power of
detachment in some English exiles is extraordinary.
This honest gentleman was snorting with fury and
contempt because a very famous foreign author
had just given a lecture in the town; and this
benighted foreigner had outraged the primary laws
of the cosmos by wearing a white shirt-front,
though it was only five o'clock in the afternoon.
Now, I have not lived in Italy for fifteen years;
but I had not lived in London up to the age of
fifteen without hearing from somebody who knew
something about the world that white shirt-fronts
do not mean the same thing in Europe that they
mean in England. They do not stand for evening

dress; they only stand for full dress; for formal or official dress. Sometimes, I believe, they are worn by students going in for important examinations. When I had a private audience with the Pope, I wore what we call evening dress, though it was eleven o'clock in the morning. I did the same when I had an interview with Mussolini. It is simply the recognized uniform worn to express any sort of special respect for a special occasion; as Englishmen would wear Court dress at Court. But in England it has had a particular evolution and adaptation to a particular social purpose, doubtless for various local reasons. I suspect that one cause was the common habit of the English gentry of hunting and riding for long stretches; so that when they returned weary and muddy they naturally wished to change into something, and fell into the habit of changing into full ceremonial dress.

But there is nothing central or essential about this particular use of the thing. What we call evening dress has nothing about it especially suggestive of the evening. Rather, we might say, its black and white effects suggest the strong light and shade of broad daylight, and might be a fitting uniform for noon. Anyhow, it is not specially suggestive of twilight. So poetical a people as the English, if they had wanted to invent vestments full of the subdued glow of the gloaming, could surely have invented something richer and softer than that. A single gleam of golden shirt-front, a

touch of crimson tie, and the rest sinking into
dimmer shades of purple and violet trousers would
be more suggestive of the tints of an English sunset.
But the English did not invent evening dress to
symbolize the evening, because the English did not
invent evening dress at all. They took some modi-
fication of the general European form of full dress;
and, being rather specially fond of comfort and
cleanliness and such eccentricities, they made it a
sort of luxury to change in the evening. There is
nothing wrong about that, and there may be much
that is right about it. The customs which I have
conjectured to be connected with it are quite good
customs in their way. It is a very jolly thing to
ride horses; it is even a laudable thing to please
ladies. But it is only one of the ten thousand good
customs there are in the world; and it is a local
variation of something that existed before in a
more general and formal form. But so completely
had my friend succeeded in living spiritually in
Surbiton, while living physically in Florence, that
he had never so much as heard in all those fifteen
years that foreigners wore shirt-fronts on a different system of etiquette. He regarded the poor
foreign gentleman as some sort of impossible swaggering snob, whose raging vanity and vulgarity
could not be restrained from beginning to put on
evening dress immediately after lunch. This seems
to me a very extraordinary state of things; very
comic and rather tragic, in these days when so much

may depend upon Christian nations understanding each other.

I do not want the English or anybody else to be international in the sense of cosmopolitan. Christendom has developed in a national form; and men who have no patriotism are not inside Europe but rather outside it. A Frenchman who does not love France, an Englishman who does not love England, is a bad European and not a good European. He has no sympathy with some of the strongest motives of all other Europeans. But the case I mean is something quite different from the case for cosmopolitanism. Indeed, the case is exactly the other way. Bigotry of the kind I mean does not arise from feeling vividly the points of difference, but rather from not realizing that there can be any differences at all. It does not come from valuing a local thing as local, but from exactly the opposite error of supposing that it must be universal.

The English are not Nationalist enough. They love their nation; but they love it almost without knowing that it is a nation. And even when such an emotion is both natural and noble, there is always some miscalculation or confusion when things are not loved strictly according to their own nature; as there are people who cannot be persuaded to love a dog as a dog or a child as a child. An attachment to particular variations of custom or humour is weakened when it is watered down to a sort of false generalization. Now, the common English error is excellently illustrated in that trivial topic of dress clothes. The English do not say, "This is the English way and a jolly good way it is." They say, "This is the only way; and it is a curious fact that, wherever we go in our travels, we notice that it is only the English who really observe it." Instead of saying that their custom is a good custom, or even that it is the best custom, they say that nobody except themselves seems to bother about observing the custom which every one must admit is the best. And this blunder comes from blindness to national differences, rather than from exaggeration of them. It does not come from being too vivid, but rather from being too vague, about the difference between an Englishman and an Italian.

I am inclined to think that this vague prejudice is now much more dangerous than a more violent prejudice. It is not the old problem of softening almost savage prejudices in the provinces of Europe; it is not that Englishmen have any particular tendency to hate Frenchmen or Germans; for the English have very little natural tendency to hate anything. It may well be said that there are many things, such as some of their own abuses and falsifications, which they do not hate enough. The nature of the error lies in this: that they never by any chance think of an English thing as a variation of a European thing. Only too often they think of a European thing as a mere misapplication of an

English thing. If they saw a portrait of Francis I in a wide flat cap and a square-cut jacket, they would not unnaturally say that Francis I was dressed like Henry VIII. The trouble is that they never think, even experimentally or fancifully, that Henry VIII was dressed like Francis I. There would always remain with them a shadowy, fantastic idea that Louis Napoleon had borrowed the top-hat of Lord Palmerston, and that it could not possibly be the other way round. They do not distinguish, for instance, between certain modern inventions which really did originate in this country and others which have equally certainly originated in other countries. They think of a railway train as an English thing, and they are right; for it did actually spread from England to Europe. But they would hardly think of a motor-car as a French thing, though it actually originated in the same sense in France and spread to England. Even the familiar name of the Italian inventor would hardly make them think of wireless sets as Italian, although the word "Marconi" is almost a synonym for "wireless." True, for some of us it is still a synonym for other things.

ONE of the queer puzzles of modern politics might
be stated in this way. That when power was
permanent, it was always reminded that it was
passing; but when power was really supposed
to be passing, it was actually treated as if it
were permanent. In the days when kings could
really cut off anybody's head, they were incessantly informed by seers and sages that they themselves would soon be cut off. When they were real
despots with the power of life and death, there
were real prophets or satirists who told them that
death would be the end of their own life. But nobody ever said this, since democratic and liberal
ideas were supposed to prevail in the State. Nobody told the really temporary ruler that he was
temporary, or even that he was temporal. From
the beginning of historic things, and almost of
prehistoric things, there has been this warning
against worldly power. The Egyptian rulers
feasted with the skeleton at the feast. The Roman
conqueror, in his triumph, had a slave towering
behind his chariot and whispering "Remember that
you are mortal." The mediæval Norman king of
Sicily, as described in the story, was reminded by

the religious service that God had put down the mighty from their seat. The later mediæval princes were familiar with the habit of feasting under frescoes and mosaics of the Dance of Death, which showed a squalid skeleton carrying away kings in a bag. Through the whole of the four thousand years of our recorded history in Europe, Pagan and Christian, has sounded that sublime and subversive dirge—

> The glories of our blood and state
> Are shadows, not substantial things.

The very Court chaplains of the great French monarchy preached before the *Roi Soleil,* telling him that even his own sun would set. And then, by some quite unaccountable change, there came with the nineteenth century the notion of men talking as if they alone could live in an everlasting sunrise.

Nobody ever did these things to modern politicians. Nobody insisted on a skeleton sitting at Table A, on the right hand of the Lord Mayor introducing the Prime Minister. Nobody insisted on the large and terrific Toast-Master, after he had, in a voice of thunder, craved silence for the Right Honourable the Lord Bundlebury, K.G., K.C.M.G., leaning forward and in a low and vibrant voice hissing in the ear of that statesman: "Remember that you are mortal." Even in the days of constitutional monarchy, pulpit orations before the king do not remind us so much of funeral orations over the king. But in the case of politicians, as distinct from kings, the whole tradition of this truth has totally disappeared. No artist covers walls and ledges with decorative designs of Death carrying away Cabinet Ministers in a bag. No poet writes a mournful ode about newspaper proprietors, even when they wear coronets, with the ancient burden—

> The glories of our scoop and stunt
> Are shadows, not substantial things.

With the nineteenth century there came in a new and unnatural optimism about the duration of earthly fashions, political and even philosophical. Shakespeare, living under the Tudors, who could (and did) kill anybody they wanted to kill, could write in a detached way about man who, "dressed in a little brief authority, plays such fantastic tricks before high heaven as make the angels weep." The modern elected politician is in theory dressed in even more brief authority. And, heaven knows, he plays fantastic tricks enough; not only to make the angels weep, but even possibly to make the angels laugh. And yet no poets or dramatists of the last hundred years ever wrote in that fashion about him. Nobody ever told the popular Prime Minister that he also would pass away, not even six months before he did pass away. Nobody ever told politicians that they would be food for worms, even when the worms were almost indistinguishable from the politicians. That long, literary lamentation and protest against the powers of this world, which has gone on through the ages, and includes a thousand things from the *Magnificat* to *Gulliver's Travels,* did in some strange way stop with the epoch of parliamentary rule, which was supposed to be popular rule. Of all the questions asked by hecklers at a political meeting to support a parliamentary candidate, I gravely and grievously doubt whether any man ever rose from the back benches, a sad and saturnine figure, to say: "Mr. Chairman, I should like to ask our candidate whether it has ever occurred to him that he will one day die."

All this, I fear, will sound very fantastic in modern ears; and even especially in parliamentary ears, which are often rather long ears. But I do sincerely believe that it contains the essential point about the essential evil that has ruined parliamentary institutions, considered as popular institutions. That sort of optimism is alone enough to cut men off from common human happiness. All the old rulers of mankind, in one way or another, were steeped in this grand and tragic tradition. The king was constantly reminded that he would die; the priest existed to remind him that he would die; the soldier was, by hypothesis, a man permanently ready to die. But this sense of the mortal brotherhood of mortals in some way disappeared when the modern world began to teach brotherhood. Since that time every General Election has been regarded as a Last Judgment. Since then, every democratic experiment has been a New Deal. People were taught to look only to the future, or at least every part of it except their own future. They were taught never to look at the past, because the past had borne unbroken testimony to this element of time and change. And that is the real reason why the world has been, as they say just now, disappointed with democracy. There is no necessary depression or despair about democracy. What is depressing is optimism. There is nothing false in the idea of the equality of man; but there is something utterly false in denying the thing in which men are most obviously equal, which is death.

If the modern democratic experiment had been a mediæval democratic experiment—if it had been, for that matter, a Moslem democratic experiment—it would not have made this mistake or got into this mess. The nuisance of the nineteenth century was that it tried to combine the common sense of the fellowship that men have in common, which is all perfectly sound and true, with an artificial expectation of Utopia; an entirely new notion that everything that was bad yesterday, and worse to-day, will inevitably be right to-morrow. That large and ludicrous illusion has nothing to do with the idea of men feeling their fellow-men as fellows

—or even as good fellows. It was an illusion of the intellectuals, who happened to be prigs and dictated the Victorian idea of progress. There is nothing wrong with democracy; there is nothing wrong with the people ruling, except what is wrong with anybody out of the people ruling; what is wrong is forgetting that people are only people. They will make mistakes, as you and I make mistakes; and as all our superiors, the supermen, the dictators, the makers of modern systems, will also make them. There was only one supreme modern mistake, which was that men forgot for a hundred years that they are liable to make mistakes.

I CONFESS that to me the celebration of the
Centenary of William Morris seems to have been
both inadequate and inappropriate. The world
seems to be divided in this respect into two
very unequal sections. The first are those who
owe everything to Morris and have forgotten him.
The second are those who owe nothing to Morris
but still desire to claim him. They claim him
mostly on the excuse of the word "Socialist"; a word
which was not really very applicable to him, and
is now pretty well applicable or inapplicable to
anybody. Morris certainly called himself a Socialist; but that hardly seems sufficient reason for
people of a totally opposite type calling him a
Communist; in the face of the quite different and
quite definite modern meaning of Communism.
Mr. Middleton Murry makes what I cannot but
think a delicate insinuation that the conversion of
a literary man like himself to Communism is more
or less comparable to the conversion of the older
literary man to Socialism. But it is precisely by
the test of literature, that is the test of imagination,
that it is quite impossible to get the two things
into the same picture. It would be difficult to

maintain that Milton was a belated mediæval ballad-monger, caring only for the rude old rhymed ballads and loathing the influence of classical dignity and a stately style. It would be difficult to maintain that Coleridge was a cold and mechanical imitator of Pope, concentrated on wit and reason and utterly hostile to vision and imagination. It would be hard to represent Walt Whitman as caring for nothing except the classical cameos of Landor. But it would be much harder than any of these, as an effort of imagination, to imagine William Morris worshipping modern machinery as the highest form of "rhythm," in accordance with the ugly Proletarian art of the modern Bolshevists. Of course, when once a man is dead, you can say anything you choose about what he would have done if he were alive. Dead men tell no tales and contradict no tales; and there is nothing to prevent the tale-bearers from writing a post-mortem sequel full of amazing conversions and contradictions. But a man has just as much right to say that Shelley would have become a True Blue Tory and High Churchman, or that Hurrell Froude, of the Oxford Movement, would soon have turned into a Radical secularist of the Manchester School, as to say that the human, historical William Morris, as he really was, would have tolerated for ten seconds the vast industrial materialism of the Five-Year Plan.

The great achievement of William Morris was

this: that he nearly convinced a whole generation that the nineteenth century was not normal. In this he was years and years ahead of the Communists of the twentieth century, who still really believe that the nineteenth century was normal. Otherwise, they would not believe that all this nightmare of machinery is normal; still less that it is new. When the Bolshevist of to-day tells us that through the impersonal power and massed material force of machinery we shall reach a more rational civilization, he is talking exactly as Mr. Gradgrind, Mr. Bounderby, Mr. Podsnap, and Mr. Bottles talked in fiction; and exactly as Sir Robert Peel, Mr. Roebuck, Mr. Bright, and Mr. Brown, of Victoria Villas, West Brixton, talked in real life. Both existed under the superstition or delusion that machines and machine-made goods are a part of the necessities of a humane culture or a common comfortable life. The Marxians, of course, have got all these notions, partly from Marx, who was a nineteenth-century man if ever there was one, and partly from the accident by which Russia was necessarily nearly a century behind the other nations, and was still looking for a panacea in what the rest of us have already found to be a quack medicine. But Morris was far ahead of Marx. Morris was not a nineteenth-century man; or he was the one nineteenth-century man who really saw through the nineteenth century.

It is true that the most widespread effect of

his revolution was in the comparatively superficial matter of domestic ornament or personal adornment. But precisely because the example is simple, or even because it is superficial, it serves as a very clear and popular example to prove the fact. What was the matter with the nineteenth century, at the height of its commercial triumph, was precisely this illusion of normality in a thing thoroughly abnormal. The satirists of the Victorian merchant said that he was commonplace. But the satirists were even more kind to him than his flatterers. What was the matter with the Victorian merchant was, not that he was commonplace, but that he thought he was commonplace. And in this he was totally in error. He had got it fixed in his mind that wearing a chimney-pot hat, an ugly pair of trousers, an ugly pair of whiskers was sane and sensible and even ordinary. Compared with these, he thought that wearing a cocked hat or a cloak or a turban or a sombrero, or a neat pair of knee-breeches or a fierce pair of moustaches were all various eccentricities, like the fancies of a fancy-dress ball. He did not realize that he looked much funnier to the fantastic foreigners than the fantastic foreigners looked to him. And, as it was with his dress, so it was with his furniture and even his architecture; with the repp curtains and red plush sofas and bad pictures in heavy gilded frames. It would have been all right if he had said, "This is my taste"; but what he did say was, "This is everybody's common sense." Now, to upset a public prejudice like that is much more difficult than to murder an emperor or seize the government offices of a republic.

Morris is still occasionally reproached with the fact that he largely selected, as his counter-example of a more common and human background, the stretch of centuries that we call the Middle Ages. But in truth, one does not need even to be a mediævalist in order to see that he was right to choose the mediæval. If, for instance, he had tried to make his revolution a return to the classic freedom of Greek and Pagan antiquity, his revolution would have been no revolution at all. It was precisely from the too-crushing convention derived from classic antiquity that art in his time had suffered most. For him it was not only the antique, but the antiquated; even in the ordinary recent sense of the old-fashioned. It was already the mere conventionalism of the Academy and the Academy School. It could not be really the Renaissance of the Hellenic at the very moment when it was the death and dregs of the Renaissance. But there is a further subtlety not sufficiently noticed. Few have really looked quite straight at the Greek beauty of the Gorgon; and most of them have been turned to stone. The Renaissance of the sixteenth century saw it, quite as much as did the Pre-Raphaelitism of the nineteenth century, in the mirror of its own mood. Morris did deal with Jason as well as John Ball; but he saw Jason through a mediæval medium. So did the Victorian classicists see Jason through a modern medium. A Renaissance style, filtered through Rubens and Reynolds, was no more Greek than a classical theme rendered by Botticelli or Burne-Jones. Both were modern versions; but the mediæval version had this advantage: that mediævalism marked a period really noted for forms of craftsmanship needed to correct the mechanism of the nineteenth century. Thus William Morris stands between two mechanical heresies; testifying that true art is always manual labour. In spite of the Victorians, it is not normal that work should be mass production. In spite of the Bolshevists, their imitators, it is not normal that it should be mass possession.

WIDOWS have always been regarded as an alarming and avenging tribe. In the background of history, back to the time of barbarism, they stand like rigid statues with uplifted arms, calling down the vengeance of heaven upon slayers and spoilers; it was especially their wrongs that the knight was pledged to vindicate when he received the accolade; it is still to the righting of their grievances that the King is bound by the Coronation Oath. They have been nobly treated in ancient tragedy and even in more recent romance; as in that story of the Highland Widow, which is always classed with Scott's worst works, apparently because it is one of his best. The atmosphere changed from tragedy to comedy, with the coming of the more comfortable sentimentality of the nineteenth century. The conception of the comic widow, as distinct from the tragic widow, a conception started long before by the arresting originality of Chaucer, touching that recurrent widow, the Wife of Bath, underwent another broadening and flattening in passing from the comedy of Chaucer to the comedy of Dickens. Tony Weller became the voice of mankind, uttering its ancient

fear of widows. And now the widow has entered
on a third phase in relation to literature: after the
tragedy of Sophocles and Scott, the comedy of
Chaucer and Dickens. The widow has become
literary herself; and reminded us that we might
have had the memoirs of Mrs. Chaucer or the auto-
biography of Mrs. Dickens. Hitherto, the method
has been simple enough. As next to nothing is
known about Philippa Chaucer, and there is nothing very much to be said about her, there has been
a mysterious assumption that there was nothing to
be said for her. It has been oddly assumed that
any Chaucerian jokes about wives must be jokes
against his own wife; in defiance of the obvious
fact that most of the same sort of jokes against
wives were made by mediæval clerics who had no
wives at all. On the other hand, as the wife of
Charles Dickens wrote nothing to speak of about
the story of her life, a modern critic has been so
obliging as to write it for her, entirely out of his
own head.

But the third and most formidable phase of the
widow in literature requires special and rather
grave consideration. At least two, if not three or
four, of the wives of distinguished men of letters
recently dead have almost simultaneously published their impressions of their own and their
husbands' private lives. It is not my primary
purpose here to discuss the propriety of this new
domestic habit beyond saying that nothing would

ever induce me personally to have anything to do with it. But the deeper causes of this difference of opinion are here rather more interesting than the difference itself. For the causes seem to me to go rather deep into a new and even unnatural view of life and art. The question might be put for debate in many forms; but perhaps the simplest form of all, to which it ultimately works back, can be found in the old debating-club query of Is Life Worth Living? For there seem to be more and more people who put it to themselves, consciously or unconsciously, in the form of Is Life Worth Writing About?

In other words, it is supposed that all this publicity of self-revelation represents an interest in private life. Sometimes, it may be admitted perhaps, an excessive interest in private life. But it seems to me to indicate a lack of interest in private life. That is, it is a lack of intensity of interest in life as a thing to be lived, and a limitation of the interest to a biography as a thing to be written. If we happen to object to "the sale of Keats's love-letters by auction," as did Oscar Wilde; or to the clown and knave who would not let the bones of Shakespeare rest, as did Alfred Tennyson; or to those who would cut a man's house in two to watch him in his parlour or bedroom, as did Robert Browning . . . if you happen to express some of the regrets felt by these eminent Victorians, you will now always find yourself confronted with

one general idea. It is the idea that the love-
letters were *wasted* if they were not sold to an
illiterate millionaire from Nebraska; or that the
poet's private emotions and meditations are *wasted*
if somebody does not spy upon him walking in his
garden; or that life inside the house is *wasted* if
people outside the house know nothing about it.
And this seems to me to mean a lack of appreciation, not only of private life, but of life itself.
Literary expression is a very valuable part of
human experience; but this is making human
experience merely a part of literary expression.
And though it is done by the most refined persons,
and often from really fine motives, it seems to me
to drift unconsciously with the whole of that
modern tide of mere sale and exchange that has
been the curse of all our recent history. I do not
mean, of course, that there is any need to denounce
every woman who happens to be a widow who may
happen to write something about some man who
happens to be an artist, even if he also happens
to be her husband. It is a question of the way in
which the thing is done; and above all of the way
in which the thing is defended. And where it is
defended on the ground that anything left private
is merely buried and lost, that defence is utterly
indefensible. It does really imply that nobody has
any inner life; that human happiness is not the
need of human beings; that man is not an end in
himself, subject only to the glory of God; or, in

short, that biography was not made for man but man for biography.

What amuses me about this fallacy of the intellectual and the superior persons is how very near it is to the fallacy of the hucksters and the go-getters and the most vulgar sort of capitalist exploiters. For they hold as their chief heresy, in a coarser form, the fundamental falsehood that things are not made to be used but made to be sold. All the collapse of their commercial system in our own time has been due to that fallacy of forcing things on a market where there was no market; of continually increasing the power of supply without increasing the power of demand; or briefly, of always considering the man who sells the potato and never considering the man who eats it. And just as we need much more of the subsistence farm, or the worker who simply produces for his own consumption, so we need much more of what may be called in moral matters the subsistence family; that is, the private family that can be really excited about its own private life; the household that is interested in itself. It is all nonsense to say that such a thing is impossible. Even by the test of literature, there is a whole mass of literature which witnesses both to its actuality and to its attractiveness. But life is much more real than literature. What Stevenson called the great theorem of the livableness of life can be solved without incessant distractions either of publicity or dissipation. It cannot be conducted without reasonable holidays and changes of scene or occupation; nor can anything else. But it can certainly be conducted; and it can certainly be interesting and even exciting. Now, to suggest that a love-letter or a family joke or a secret language among children is never really important until it is edited and published, is to imply only too much of the suggestion of so many memoirs: that a man is only interesting when he is dead. For the whole world of mere stunts and scoops and trading and self-advertisement is spiritually a world utterly dead; although it is very noisy. It is, in the precise and literal meaning of the phrase, a howling wilderness.

WHEN we hear one particular word such as "Relativity" repeated about a hundred times a week, and scattered over scores of newspapers and novels and ordinary publications, we may deduce with almost practical certainty that nobody who is using the word has any notion of what it means. I do not mean merely that few of them have read about Relativity in some new and technical sense, in which it may be found necessary for explaining an abstruse theory of Professor Einstein. I do not even mean that most people are unacquainted, as they naturally are, with the various forms of ancient scepticism, dating at least from the earliest Greek philosophers, to which the term "Relativity" might be reasonably applied. I mean that people do not consider even the common meaning of the word that has become so common. They do not realize even what they themselves mean, or have always meant, by the word considered as a part of the English language. It is as if there were suddenly a universal mania for talking about hats, without the faintest memory that they had ever had anything to do with heads; or as if everybody were extravagantly excited about cats,

while nobody knew whether they were the same
as crocodiles.

In the English language, as in any national
language capable of normal logic, anything relative
is relative to something positive. We describe it
by saying it stands in a certain relation to something already known. This is so in the practical
popular use of "relative" or "relation." You may
say with gloom, "I'm going to stay with relations";
or you may say with complacency, "Admiral Sir
Caradoc Valencourt Vere de Vere is a relative of
mine"; or you may say in a Parliamentary manner
(if you are in the House of Lords, as I assume that
you are), "My noble relative will find it difficult to
reconcile the baseness and trickery of his treatment
of the pickled-onion problem with his professions
as an Englishman and a Christian"; or you may
say sardonically, "I suppose Mrs. Boulger-Buckett
regards us as her poor relations." But in all these
cases, however different the emotion, there is no
difference in the reason, as it defines the nature of
a relation. In all cases the other objects are
regarded as being in various relations to a fixed
object; and in this case the object is what is called
the subject. In other words, for a large proportion
of fallen humanity the fixed point is oneself; and
this is reasonable, in so far as there is a fixed certainty of the reality of oneself. You do really
know that you really exist; even in some wild
mood in which Admiral Sir Caradoc Vere de Vere

might seem to be only a beautiful dream; or Mrs. Boulger-Buckett one of those dark fancies that flit across the brain upon the borderland of nightmare. You therefore speak of them as relative to yourself; if only because you know more about yourself than you know about them. But when people begin to talk about universal relativity, as if everything were as relative as everything else, so that presumably the very notion of relativity is itself relative, only relative to nobody knows what, they are simply knocking the bottom out of the world and the human brain, and leaving a bottomless abyss of bosh. You say, with airy grace, that Sir Caradoc Vere de Vere is a relation of yours. You do not say he is a relation, as if it were a profession or a post or a position in itself. There is no such thing as a relation wandering about the world with nobody to be related to. And if your philosophy talks of relations in that sense, the philosopher will decide that they are very poor relations indeed.

A somewhat similar use has been made lately of the word "hypothesis." There has been a correspondence in *The Times* about the nature of belief, or unbelief, or incidentally of make-believe. This was enriched by a somewhat pompous letter from a very superior person, who said he was entirely Modern; and proceeded to set forth as much as he could understand of the early sceptical sages of ancient Hellas, to whom I have referred; and proceeded to adorn the theme with things so exclusively modern as the exact meaning of dialectic in the dialogues of Plato. But his scepticism was much more archaic than Plato; indeed it was the sort of nihilistic nonsense that Socrates existed largely in order to chaff out of existence. The form it took here was the repeated suggestion that a Modern person cannot believe in anything except as a hypothesis. In other words, that he cannot believe in anything at all. For you cannot believe in a hypothesis; you can only give it a fair chance to prove itself a thesis that can be believed.

Now, even the Modern Man is not necessarily a madman; and this would hopelessly ruin and destroy every modern use of hypothesis; especially the whole scientific idea of a hypothesis holding the field. It would merely mean ensuring that what is called a working hypothesis would not work. For a man could not even construct a hypothesis if he could only construct it out of hypothetical things. There can be no hypothesis if there is nothing but hypothesis. Anybody can see that, if he will merely consider any actual example. For instance, the Darwinian theory of Natural Selection was a hypothesis; and it is still only a hypothesis. Popular science insists on repeating that it is a hypothesis that has been confirmed; with the result that responsible science is more and more treating it as a hypothesis that has been abandoned. But it can be quite rightly treated as a reasonable hypothesis, by anybody who believes in it, if he can support it with other things in which he believes; or preferably things in which everybody believes. He is quite entitled to say, "We suggest that a monkey, probably living in a tree, became the ancestor of a man, apparently living in a cave, by a process of adaptations beginning with slight varieties of feature in his family, by which it survived only in those cases where the features favoured the finding of food. It may not yet be finally confirmed by the fossils found in the rocks or the habits of the monkeys still found in the trees; but we still think it the most probable hypothesis and confidently await proof." But he could not even say that, if he were compelled to explain his suggestion in some such form as this: "We suggest that a monkey (if there are any monkeys) living in a tree (if there are any trees) became the ancestor of a man (if we may risk the speculative supposition that there is such a thing as a man) through certain variations enabling certain types to find food (granted the truth of the traditional dogma that food is favourable to life), and we look to the hypothetical fossils which may or may not be found in the hypothetical rocks which may or may not be found in the world; or to the behaviour of monkeys we cannot actually believe in, in trees we cannot actually believe in, and faintly trust to a larger hope that something may somehow make some sense out of the whole caboodle. But even if something does happen, by which this hypothesis seems to fit in better with all the other hypotheses, we can never believe it even at the end as anything except the hypothesis that it was at the beginning; because the good kind gentleman in *The Times* tells us it would not be Modern."

This would be enough to show the futility of this relative and sceptical style of thinking, even for the pure purposes of thought. It is only because the reflection adds something to the fun of the thing, that I even refer to the unthinkable effects which such thought would have upon action. One thing is at least certain whatever our national or international views: that, in practice, over large parts of Europe that sort of scepticism has already perished under terrible tests. The world resounds with iron convictions, some sinister, some sublime, but all only too ready to bring forth the fruits of martyrdom or of murder. We also may yet suffer or defy; and I fear *The Times* sceptic will discover that he is not so very Modern.

MANY modern debates are still revolving round the old question, even if it is put in new forms, which was generally expressed in the form: "Can you alter human nature?" Like many such questions, which were at least accepted as questions, whatever might be the answer, the question was wrongly asked, even if it was rightly answered. In strict logic and philosophy, if you could actually alter the nature of human beings, they would cease to be human beings. So you could not really point to them as human beings whose nature had been altered. It would be better to put the question in some such form as this: "What are the elements in humanity which are changeable; and what are the elements that are unchangeable, if any of them are unchangeable?" But the question has almost always been debated between two extreme types of humanity, neither of whom could be said to specialize in logic or philosophy.

At the one extreme there was the blustering, not to say blundering, type of Tory who answered almost any proposal for the improvement of social law and custom by shouting at the reformer: "You can't change human nature." If, for instance, a reformer proposed to resist the concentration of capital in combines and corners, the dear old gentleman would declare that nothing could stop the growth of monopolies and money-rings, because we could not alter human nature. This only serves to prove that he was himself singularly ignorant of human nature, if only because he was singularly ignorant of human history. By a queer irony, the Conservative who thought he was a traditionalist was defending the most modern of innovations against all the old traditions of mankind. And the joke of it is that in this he was himself a living proof that you can alter human nature, if you call that sort of thing altering human nature. His moral theory was entirely modern, and was in flat contradiction to the moral theory that is really ancient. Most of his ancestors regarded making a corner simply as a crime, like that of cutting a throat or picking a pocket. Forestallers, as our fathers called them, were often put in a pillory, or even hanged on a gallows, to stop them from doing what he declares they cannot be stopped from doing. If he regards monopoly with patience or approval, while his fathers regarded it with fury and condemnation, that is alone sufficient evidence of a change in human nature, in the sense of human theories about human nature. In fact, that sort of man regards the peculiar vices of the new age as the permanent vices of every age; that is, when his complacency does not go further, and regard them as virtues rather than vices. If that is what is meant by change in the nature of man, it is quite certain that we could change a monopolist society into an anti-monopolist society, as we have already changed an anti-monopolist society into a monopolist society. The real answer is that this sort of thing is not really a change in the nature of man. It is simply an unchanging quality in the nature of man that he is fickle, moody, and one-sided; that he stresses now one point in morals and now another, neglects one virtue and then goes on in progressive triumph to neglect another; that he is overpowered by whatever is recent and generally ignorant of whatever is remote; and, above all, that he mistakes experience for existence, and supposes that what he sees is all that there is to see. There certainly is in human nature this changing quality; and it is an unchanging quality.

On the other side, and at the other extreme, is the eager evolutionist or progressive who cries aloud: "But we can alter human nature. We have altered human nature." I happened to meet a young man of this type recently, a rising and promising man of letters, who used almost exactly these words, and followed them by the (to me) still more intriguing words: "In the past, people used to burn witches, to own slaves, to persecute heretics, and all the rest. Don't you admit that human nature must have changed?" To which I answered: "No; it has not changed; it has only been changeable." That is, the young gentleman ignored exactly what the old gentleman ignored: that there is all the difference in the world between a man liking different things, like a man, and the man ceasing to be like a man.

I have not the slightest difficulty in imagining the world of the future taking a turn which would bring back the fact, if not the form, of witch-hunting and slavery and the persecution of heresies. These things might grow out of entirely modern things, without any conscious reference to the ancient things. For instance, Spiritualism is in origin a modern thing; and the desire for a certain sort of scientific system of psychical phenomena is certainly a modern thing. If Spiritualism did become a world-wide religion, it is not hard to see that divisions would begin between the more and the less scientific people. Some would denounce a medium as a fraud, while others would still cling to him as a seer.

For Spiritualism differs from most religions in this: that its scriptures are not a scroll or book recognized from the beginning; they are potentially *all* the scribblings of all the planchettes and spirit-pens in a thousand private houses. It is inevitable that some disputes should arise about which come from good spirits, which from evil spirits, which from evil men. The moment the element of evil spirits enters, you have the material for horrible panics about their power and their picked instruments. In a few centuries, a more sombre psychic sect would be quite capable of regarding others as diabolists to be cast out like devils. Modern mystics have said some extraordinary things in that way. A Spiritualist whose book was published when I was a boy, a certain Dr. Anna Kingsford, proudly proclaimed that she had killed, not to say murdered, men by an act of will, when they differed from her on certain points, as on vivisection. That spirit is not far from that of mystics killing each other, as agents of the mystery of iniquity. Supposing that large parts of civilization turned to that sort of mysticism, I do not think it would be long before we had something resembling the war upon witches. Whether it will take that turn, of course, I cannot tell; I hope not. But nobody, at this moment, can tell what turn the spiritual history of the future will take.

Of the other two things my friend thought unthinkable in a changed humanity, one can speak much more positively. It is inadequate to say that they might be done in the future; it would be truer to say that they are being done in the present. There are many indications of men going back to everything connected with Slavery, except the name of Slavery. Half the new systems of the hour are now dealing in conscripted labour, in forced labour of every kind, in which there is no pretence of a free contract. Strictly speaking, if you keep private property and forbid strikes, or even individual refusal of work, you do establish slavery. You even establish a Fugitive Slave Law. But my young friend, his eyes fixed on the future, had apparently not noticed anything that has been beginning in the last few years. He had been taught that human nature had changed; he had not been told that it has changed again.

As for persecution, it has become a grim joke in the case of the Jews; nor is it less persecution if we call it the persecution of a race and not the persecution of a religion. The truth is that the whole of the old original theory of persecution has been openly proclaimed and practised, not in the old, but in the new political systems. Doubtless those political systems deal even more in political persecution than in religious persecution. But that does not make them less persecuting, but more. The whole point of the last political theory is that sectional parties and programs must be forcibly effaced; that the opposition press must be abolished, and only one party allowed. I am not saying that there is nothing to be said for persecution. It is a much more profound problem than progressives have ever found out. But it does measure the exact sense and degree in which humanity does change, that it should disappear in the nineteenth century to reappear in the twentieth.

I AM happy to say that there seems to be a real revival of interest in history; but, oddly enough, it does not mainly express itself in histories. It seems to express itself almost entirely in biographies.

There are, of course, several distinguished exceptions; it is good news that so great a scholar as Mr. H. A. L. Fisher has published a History of Europe; and I think that few more compact and convincing pieces of work have been done than Mr. Belloc's abridged History of England. But the fashion of the moment, or the feature of the movement, seems to me to be the publication of separate monographs on separate historical characters. We do not see, for instance, at least in any prominent example, the reappearance of the old full and formal narrative of the great national legend of the Cavaliers and Roundheads; a complete history of the Civil War, with its causes and consequences, set out like a section of a long, complete history of the nation. What we do see on every bookstall, and in every bookcase, is a number of new biographies of the men who once figured almost entirely in such histories. We find that Mr. Belloc writes a book on Charles I; that Mr.

Buchan writes a book on Oliver Cromwell; that Mr. Belloc writes another book on Oliver Cromwell; and that another historical student has just written another book on the great Earl of Strafford. I have no doubt that, if I looked through the literary lists in a more systematic manner than it is within the power of my patience and virtue to look through anything, I should find that somebody had written a book on Sir Henry Vane; that somebody else had written a book on Lord Falkland; that somebody else had made a most learned study of Clarendon, but had not imitated Clarendon in writing a history of the Civil War. Now I come to recall it, there was recently a book, if not two books, on John Hampden; and I trust and believe there will always be any number of books on John Milton.

Between them, one would suppose these books would pretty well cover the whole ground that could be covered by a complete history. But, in fact, as compared with a complete history, any number of them must still remain incomplete. There is no conspectus of all these contrasted characters, seen together in the light of the same mind or general philosophy of history; and some of them naturally contradict each other so flatly as to lead rather to confusion than conclusion. A man has some reason for selecting the subject of another man; and the chances are that his reason, even if perfectly reasonable, will be highly personal; and sometimes personal to the point of being perverse. There is always a possible association of a monograph with a monomania. And though many of these books, and especially those I have mentioned, are filled with a real sense of history which goes far beyond mere biography, in the sense of mere gossip, these personal studies may easily involve a certain amount of mere scandal; sometimes involving a temptation to mere slander. Anyhow, either in the best examples or the worst, we can hardly find in biography a substitute for history; or be completely satisfied by looking at the program for the *dramatis personæ* as an alternative to seeing the play.

I wonder nobody has ever written a History of the Histories of England. The historians would themselves be characters in a very entertaining play. Summaries of their treatment of the same subject would have something of the unexpected variety of the versions of the same story in Browning's experiment of *The Ring and the Book*. Anyhow, the historians would be very vivid characters; some of them, to tell the truth, rather comic characters. And we should possess a rather important outline of the actual evolution of political thought or patriotic sentiment, through periods which are none the less important to our national destiny because nearly all of us have forgotten all about them. A very good example of what would strike us as a new truth, merely by being a neglected truth, can be found in the case of David

Hume, when he wrote as a historian and not as a philosopher. Huxley revived Hume as a philosopher, in the days of his own fight for Agnosticism and quarrel with Comtism, calling the Scotch sceptic "that prince of agnostics." But I rather doubt whether Huxley would have bothered much about Hume as a historian; for Huxley was very Victorian in many ways, including the Victorian virtues. And, by his time, the whole Victorian world had undergone a profound change in the whole attitude towards history; a change that has rather falsified the whole perspective of the history of history, even of history so recent as Hume's.

Macaulay, after all, was something of a magician, even if he was also something of a cheap and popular conjurer. He was a romancer rather than a liar; at the worst, he was a romancer as well as a liar. That is, he was sincere in his enjoyment of romance, even where it departed furthest from reality. And he did do what the poets can do, though it was said to be what the gods themselves could not do. He did change the past; he did throw a retrospective glamour over the past of his own Puritan and Parliamentary party; a light that looked like broad daylight, but which had not really shone upon it in its own day. There was a case for the Puritans; but it was a Puritan case. There is still a case for a few fanatics who drink to the Immortal Memory of William of Orange, but it is a fanatical case. It is ending very much as it

began, and as it continued to be up to the moment
when the magic of Macaulay made it look like mere
practical politics or the religion of all sensible men.
I mean that, while there was a true enthusiasm in
the seventeenth-century sects, it was a sectarian
enthusiasm. We may perfectly well sympathize with
the heroic virtue of a Brownite or the martyrdom of
a Muggletonian, but it must be as we sympathize
with a dancing dervish or a wild prophet in the
wilderness; and that was about the best that the bulk
of England ever felt for the very best of the Puritans.
The English, as the English, thought about them as
the Romans thought about the Zealots; as the
Rationalists thought about the Methodist preachers.
One result of this was that the common-sense—or,
if you will, commonplace—opinion of the country,
for most of the time, was rather Royalist than
Roundhead. It was not in the least necessary to be
a romantic Cavalier, an old-world Jacobite, a High
Churchman, or even a High Tory, in order to be a
Royalist. Again and again we find that a Rationalist
was a Royalist. Hobbes was a Rationalist, hating
every trace and tradition of the old religious sentiment. But Hobbs was a Royalist, in the sense that
his despotic theory of the State involved the implica-
tion of a royal despot. Indeed, Hobbes was a Hitlerite, and his whole theory of the Totalitarian State
turns on a pivot of personal government. Hume
was a Rationalist; but in his History of England he
was a Royalist.

The most famous or fashionable of the recent monographs is the *Marlborough* of Mr. Winston Churchill. The author has to sacrifice the Whig historian to the Whig hero. I do not share Mr. Churchill's innocent and child-like piety in the matter of his trust in Marlborough, but I entirely share his distrust of Macaulay. But the matter in which Macaulay has most falsified the past is that I have mentioned; the fashion of supposing that the solid sense of the nation was solid for the Puritans and the Parliament men, with nothing against it but a chivalric but childish memory of the past. Down to very late indeed, it was still the Roundhead who was the crank and the Cavalier who was the regular guy. Dr. Johnson was a Jacobite suspected of being out in the '45; but, right or wrong, he was a more solid and sensible sort of Englishman than Horace Walpole worshipping the Regicides and the death-warrant of Charles I. But the test is Hume. He would have seemed a horrible atheist to the doctor; but he, too, was a Royalist; because he seemed to himself a sensible man.

I HAVE never quite understood the phrase that comparisons are odious; but anybody can see that even the very best of comparisons is only comparatively complimentary. A literal interpretation could turn most compliments into insults. It would not do to treat the poet as a botanist when he says "My love is like the red, red rose." There are roses which would suggest rather too apoplectic a complexion and be rough on the lady. There are ladies of whom we might say that it was rough on the rose. The line in the modern version of "Annie Laurie," "Her neck is like the swan," always suggested to me a very startling and somewhat alarming alteration in the human form; but I believe that this line was a fake put in by the false modesty of somebody who was shocked by the beautiful simplicity of the older version. But there is another sense of the word "comparative" in which it is liable to another somewhat parallel abuse or error. It is that grammatical classification of a thing in the three degrees of positive, comparative, and superlative; as illustrated in the bright little boy who gave the extension of an adverb in the form of "Ill; worse; dead." It will be noted that this, though founded on highly practical experience, is not exact as an example of grammatical logic.

Now, there are a great many phrases used in practice as comparatives which are not nearly so truly comparative as the triad of the little boy. I mean that many people suppose one thing to be an extension of another thing or an excess of another thing when it is really a totally different thing; and sometimes almost a contrary thing. For instance, some people have an instinctive itch of irritation against the word "authority." Either they suppose that authority is a pompous name for mere bullying, or else, at the best, they think that mere bullying is an excess of authority. But bullying is almost the opposite of authority. Tyranny is the opposite of authority. For authority simply means right; and nothing is authoritative except what somebody has a right to do, and therefore is right in doing. It often happens in this imperfect world that he has the right to do it and not the power to do it. But he cannot have a shred of authority if he merely has the power to do it and has not the right to do it. If you think any form of mastery unjust, it is enough to say that you do not like injustice; but there is no need to say that you do not like authority. For injustice, as such, cannot have any authority at all. Moreover, a man can only have authority by admitting something better than himself; and the bully does not get his claim from anybody but himself. It is not a question, therefore, of there being authority, and then tyranny, which is too much authority; for tyranny is no authority. Tyranny means too little authority; for though, of course, an individual may use wrongly the power that may go with it, he is in that act disloyal to the law of right, which should be his own authority. To abuse authority is to attack authority. A policeman is no longer a policeman when he is bribed privately to arrest an innocent man; he is a private criminal. He is not exaggerating authority; he is reducing it to nothing.

Another example of the false comparative, which is really not a comparative but a contrary, is the distinction between avarice and thrift. Here, again, it is of course possible for an individual to pass from one to the other; but it is only by violating the other, not by exaggerating it. The two things are really opposites; but things do sometimes produce their opposites. Love may turn to hate; a man may begin by wanting to marry a woman and end by wanting to murder her. But love is none the less the opposite of hate; and even our most advanced thinkers would hardly say that marriage is the same as murder. A man, profligate in youth, may so poison himself as to become Puritan in old age. But the reaction is none the less a reaction because it is a morbid and exaggerated reaction. In the same way a thrifty man may turn into a miser, but in turning into a miser he is ceasing to be a thrifty man. He is most

emphatically not becoming more of a thrifty man.
A miser is a man who is intercepted and misled in
his pursuit of thrift and betrayed into turning to
the pursuit of money. Madness of that sort always
haunts the life of man, as a possible temptation
and perversion. Idolatry is always a danger to the
soul, and idolatry is the worship of the instrument.
A man who thinks he is justified in drawing the
sword for justice may be tempted of the devil and
come to worship not the justice but the sword.
That is what happened to poor Nietzsche, leading
him to write that sentence which is still the motto
of Prussianism and Prussia: "You say a good cause
justifies any war; but I say a good war justifies
any cause." The peasant who follows the plough
may fall into the same temptation as the soldier
who follows the sword; but both will be turning
against their original purpose, even against their
own purpose in using their own tools. For the
peasant who thinks more of the money-bags than
he does of the flour-sacks becomes less of a peasant
in becoming more of a miser. And the real soldier
does not follow the sword, but follows the flag.

Thrift by derivation means thriving; and the
miser is the man who does not thrive. The whole
meaning of thrift is making the most of everything;
and the miser does not make anything of anything.
He is the man in whom the process, from the seed
to the crop, stops at the intermediate mechanical
stage of the money. He does not grow things to

feed men; not even to feed one man; not even to feed himself. The miser is the man who starves himself, and everybody else, in order to worship wealth in its dead form, as distinct from its living form. He is occasionally found among peasants, as the bully is occasionally found among soldiers. But in that very fact, the one is a bad peasant and the other a bad soldier. In the rather morbid modern culture of the industrial towns there has arisen a habit of denouncing both these two types, as if they always yielded to these temptations. But the towns also have their temptations; and the town critics have generally yielded to all of them. They do not understand either the peasants' sense of liberty or the soldiers' sense of loyalty; and they always assume that there is nothing but avarice in the economic independence of the one, and nothing but brutality in the militant obedience of the other. An actual experience, either of peasants or of soldiers, will soon teach anybody that the aberrations of avarice or arrogance are exceptional. The general effect of discipline on decent soldiers is to make them very pleasant companions and rather more modest and placable than the majority of men. The actual effect of thrift on most peasants is to make them inventive and intelligent in their ordinary hospitality and human intercourse. There is no difference between them and other simple and sociable human beings, except that they understand the rather important thing which economists call "economy of consumption."

A French or Flemish peasant woman will make much more out of the scraps in the kitchen, or the very weeds in the garden, than a proletarian will make out of the tinned food and advertised wares of a commercial city. But normally she will be quite as pleased, not to say proud, to put the results of her cookery before other people as if she were presiding over a fatigued cocktail-party in Mayfair. But the test of her pretensions, of her pride—one might almost say of her profession—is concerned entirely with the practical product. For the healthy-minded peasant, more than for anybody, the proof of the pudding is in the eating. She may become an unhealthy-minded peasant and think of nothing but the money; for the diseases of the soul are in the very air. Therefore, it will probably happen that every village will contain a miser— that is, a madman. But his madness has nothing to do with the sanity of thrift. Thrift in itself is always a thirst to make all things thrive, animal, vegetable, or mineral; to make them prosper and produce; to prevent their being wasted, or, in other words, destroyed. Whether particular people need to be warned of particular dangers touching the avarice that perverts thrift is a matter of moral education and religion; but the first principle is that the miser is not a more thrifty man but a much less thrifty man, for he wastes money more than a spendthrift.

THIS would be no place to inquire too closely why those bright youths who are so superior to eternity seem to be so subject and submissive to time; why they proclaim with such wild pagan gestures that they can pull down the cross; but assure us, with such anxious and agitated motions, that we cannot put back the clock. They seem to suppose that it is a sort of new religion to worship the clock; and that without even noticing that it is generally a grandfather's clock. For Time, whatever else he is, is rather an old gentleman by now; his hour-glass is a very antiquated sort of clock, and his scythe a rustic and archaic instrument quite unworthy of an exhibition of agricultural machinery. In other words, all this talk about things being suited to the times must, by its very nature, have been uttered hundreds of times before. And any one who listens in a meditative mood to the grandfather's clock will find it difficult to say that there is so very much difference between one tick and another; and may perhaps suspect that there was not quite so much difference between one time and another. I am well aware that some have hyphenated the name of Father

Time, and that calling him Space-Time may make him seem rather more spacious. But, for all that, there is a little trick of logic, like a trick of clockwork, by which the young philosopher is caught in time as in a trap. His own time closes on him with a click; as in a creepy murder story I once read, in which a man was caught and crushed in an old clock. For the fallacy which entraps him is this: that he cannot apparently resist the temptation to base his argument on the mere moment of time at which the argument takes place.

I have just read a very vivid short story about an aged *grande dame* in a country place and a young novelist whom she regarded as an upstart and a revolutionist. I hold no brief for the old lady; I entirely decline to become the grim and gaunt family solicitor who must certainly have been attached to her aristocratic family. I think she must have been a decidedly unpleasant old lady; and I think, as strongly as the strongest of youthful novelists or revolutionists, that she was stupidly priding herself upon the accident of birth. But what the young ass of a novelist could not see, and what the author of that author also could not see, was that he also was priding himself, and quite as stupidly, on the mere accident of birth. For she was only proud of having been born in a particular place; and he was only proud of having been born at a particular time. For what he said, and all he could apparently say, again and again and waving his arms about, was: "Your day is past; can't you see that your day is past? To-day is ours; to-morrow is ours," and so on; as repeatedly and relentlessly as the ticking of a clock. But this does not affect, in the smallest degree, the actual question of whether his day was worse or better than her day. If I advance the thesis that the weather on Monday was better than the weather on Tuesday (and there has not been much to choose between most Mondays and Tuesdays of late), it is no answer to tell me that the time at which I happen to say so is Tuesday evening, or possibly Wednesday morning.

It is vain for the most sanguine meteorologist to wave his arms about and cry: "Monday is past; Mondays will return no more; Tuesday and Wednesday are ours; you cannot put back the clock." I am perfectly entitled to answer that the changing face of the clock does not alter the recorded facts of the barometer. Doubtless, the old lady, when she was a young lady, declared that the present and future were hers, and that her aged aunt was very aged. But these pleasant and polite comparisons do not make it impossible to establish objective historical comparisons. And anybody is intellectually entitled to say, if he thinks so, that there was better social weather on the old woman's Monday than on the young man's Tuesday; or even on the quiet Sunday of the aged aunt. I do not say so; anyhow not about that old woman; and, as Archbishop Temple said, "I never knew her aunt." But to be rude and contemptuous to the old woman, merely on the ground that she was old, is even more unworthy of a philosopher than it is of a gentleman. And all this assumption of the superiority of the advancing hours, based on the accident of the hour that is passing, is in its nature unintelligent; in the sense in which a gross error in mathematics is unintelligent. The theory of progress may be argued; but it must be proved. It is necessary to show that certain social stages are superior to previous social stages on their own merits; and in many cases it may be possible to prove it. In some cases it is certainly possible to disprove it. But it is absurd for a young man to base his argument upon the mere fact that he began to join in the discussion in the year 1930 instead of the year 1830. That is no more valid than the fact that he joined up with his controversial companions at Turnham Green, when they had been arguing all the way from Hammersmith. The one is a mere point in time; as the other is a mere point in space; and each of them is as idle and irrelevant as any tick of the clock.

Naturally, in this tale here taken as a text, the novelist regarded himself as novel. But some study, even of the history of novelists, would have shown him that there is no such simple issue between novelty and antiquity. The novelist claims to be a realist; and he has as much right to defend realism as other novelists had to defend romanticism. But he is out by a thousand miles if he supposes that there has been a general progress from romanticism to realism; or, indeed, from anything to anything else. The great history of the great English novelists would alone be enough to show that the story was never a pure story of progress; but of rebellions and reactions; revolutions and counter-revolutions. When England began to escape from a Puritanism which forbade all romances, the great Richardson rejoiced in being able to pour out floods of tears and tenderness about the most delicate forms of love. When he had done it, the great Fielding rejoiced even more to pour out floods of derision, believing that his coarse candour and common sense was a part of enlightenment and liberty; though often concerned with less delicate forms of love.

A generation later, the great Jane Austen confessed herself disgusted by the coarseness even of Addison, and created a restrained comedy of which half the humour is its deliberate decorum. Then we went on to Dickens and Thackeray, the latter especially dismissing as barbarism what Swift and Smollett had regarded as realism, and even as liberalism. Nothing is now important about these great English novelists except that they were all great. Nobody discusses whether they were all novel; yet each in turn believed himself to be novel. Any one who goes by dates may find himself defending brutality against Richardson or prudery against Fielding. The worst argument in the world is a date. For it is actually taking as fixed the one thing that we really know is fugitive and staking all upon to-day at the moment when it is turning into yesterday. The clock-worshipper has a heavy creed of predestination; and it is only as the tavern closes that its priest cries aloud upon his god; saying, like all the sad modern sages: "Time, gentlemen, time!"

Iт is often said truly, though perhaps not often
understood rightly, that extremes meet. But the
strange thing is that extremes meet, not so
much in being extraordinary, as in being dull.
The country where the East and the West are one
is a very flat country. For such extremes are
generally extreme simplifications; and tend to a
type of generalization flattening out all real types,
let alone real personalities. Two of the dreariest
things in the world, for instance, are the way in
which the snobs among the rich talk about the
poor; and the way in which the prigs who profess
to have an economic cure for poverty themselves
talk about the poor. On the one side, we have the
class of people who are always talking about "the
lower classes," thereby proving that they belong
to a class very much lower; a class so low that it
almost deserves to be called classy. It is sufficiently
weak-minded to be proud; but this type is generally
merely purse-proud; and, as Thackeray said, "It
admires mean things meanly"; for example, it
admires itself. To hear such people talking about
servants or about working men will be enough to
send the wise and good away with a wild impulse

to make, if not a barricade, at least a butter-slide. But, curiously enough, there is something that produces almost exactly the same impression on my own feelings; and that is the pedantic way in which all people who happen to be poor are classified by some professors of Socialism or social reform; and even by some who are supposed to be working-class representatives themselves. Somehow they seem to talk about the Proletariat in exactly the same tone of voice in which the wealthier snobs talk about the lower classes. Why, for instance, is it never correct to call them "the workmen" or "the working men" but always crushingly correct to call them "the workers"? Somehow that word alone, and the ritual repetition of it, seems to discolour and drain the whole subject of any human interest. To be a workman is perhaps the noblest of all human functions; and I was delighted the other day to hear a speaker describe Mr. Eric Gill, the great sculptor, as "the first workman in the land." But the person swallowed up in these sociological generalizations is no more the last than the first. He is not a working man because he is not a man; he is not any workman anybody has ever known; he is not the funny Irish bricklayer you talked to when you were a little boy; he is not the plumber or the mysterious plumber's mate; he is not the gardener, who was rather cross; he is not the needy knife-grinder or the romantic rat-catcher. He is The

Workers; a vast grey horde of people, apparently all exactly alike, like ants; who are always on the march somewhere; presumably to the Ninth or Tenth International. And this de-humanizing way of dealing with people who do most of the practical work on which we depend, merely because they unfortunately have to do it for a wage, is really quite as irritating to anybody with any real popular sympathies as the ignorant contempt of the classes that are established and ought to be educated. And both fail upon the simple point that the most important thing about a workman is that he is a man; a particular sort of biped; and that two of him are not a quadruped nor fifty of him a centipede.

These amusing but annoying habits are but the outer expression of a social truth, which will grow more and more obviously true; but which very few people of any political or social group have yet seen to be true at all. Talking as if I were myself a wild Communist, the voice of the rough and simple masses of the poor, and therefore using the longest words I can and putting what I mean as pedantically and polysyllabically as possible, I might state the matter thus. The sociology of capitalistic industrialism began with an identification with individualism; but its ultimate organization has corresponded to a complete loss of individuality. So far so bad. But what is even worse, the sort of constructive discontent in re-

volt against it, which is still most common in the
varieties of popular opinion, has itself inherited
and carried on this indifference to individuality.
For Communism is the child and heir of Capitalism;
and the son would still greatly resemble his father
even if he had really killed him. Even if we had
what is called the Dictatorship of the Proletariat,
there would be the same mechanical monotony in
dealing with the mob of Dictators as in dealing with
the mob of wage-slaves. There would be, in practice, exactly the same sense of swarms of featureless
human beings, swarms of human beings who were
hardly human, swarms coming out of a hive,
whether to store or to sting. And when I thought
of that word, I suddenly realized why I so intensely
disliked the other words I have mentioned; for,
now I come to think of it, I believe there is one
whole section of such insects that is called "the
workers."

Upon this similarity, generally called a conflict,
between an industrial order and an equally industrial revolution, is largely founded that third
thesis, on which I have sometimes touched in this
place; the insistence on true individualism instead
of false individualism; the distribution of private
property to the individual citizens and individual
families. I am not now arguing about its political
prospects or economic effectiveness; though they
are much more hopeful than most modern people
suppose. I am thinking of it merely in relation to

the sweeping criticism and the swarming crowd;
the general tendency of people at both extremes to
simplify the problem either by contempt or by
pedantry. I mean that some of us think the Irish
bricklayer might be even funnier if he were as free
as the Irish peasant; that if the plumber always
owned his own tools, he might sometimes neglect
to leave them behind; that though a man can be
cross as well as contented with his own garden,
the fact of ownership itself tends on the whole to
contentment; and that even discontent of that
sort does not mean that a man is at once discon-
tented and indistinguishable or invisible; or reduced
to making a vague noise out of the voices of many
nameless men, like the buzzing of bees in his back
garden. For I do not believe that any human
being is fundamentally happier for being finally
lost in a crowd, even if it is called a crowd of
comrades. I do not believe that the humorous
human vanities can have vanished quite so completely from anybody as that; I think every man
must desire more or less to figure as a figure, and
not merely as a moving landscape, even if it be
a landscape made of figures. I cannot believe that
men are quite so different that any of them want
to be the same. I admit that the beginning of
men for the purposes of social protest may have
some of the justification of a just war. I even
admit that the menace of such a war may palliate
the panic-stricken arrogance of some of the ig-

norant rich, who do not know what the war is about. But I repeat that in both cases I think that habit of dealing with men in the mass, not merely on abnormal occasions, as in a war or a strike, but in normal circumstances and as a part of ordinary social speech, is a very bad way of trying to understand the human animal. There are only a few animals, and they are not human animals, who can be best judged or best employed in packs or herds. Some may compare the workers of a Communist state to a pack of wolves; I should very strongly suspect that they bear more resemblance to a flock of sheep. But neither of these animals can be said to have a very complex or entertaining type of mentality; few of us would be eager to listen, even if we could, to the flowing and continuous reminiscences of a sheep; and St. Francis seems to have been the only man who was ever on intimate terms with a wolf. It is precisely because man is the most interesting of the creatures that he finds his proper place among those creatures who dig a domestic hole or hang up an individual nest; and the disgrace of our society is not when he has not a hive or an ant hill; but when, among so many nests and holes, he has not where to lay his head.

I HAVE dared to suggest that it would be rather a good thing if educated Englishmen knew a little history. I am not worrying about uneducated Englishmen. They do know a little history; a very little history, perhaps, but genuine so far as it goes; they do remember what their father and grandfather said; in what town or village they were born; what was the tone of the society round them; and their testimony, so far as it goes, is true. Any lawyer will tell you that uneducated witnesses are much better than educated witnesses, because they have not been elaborately educated to see what is not there. But it is a bad thing that an educated man, trained to have a taste for many good things, such as music or landscape, should know nothing of the songs of his fathers, and should appreciate the landscape without appreciating the land. Now, the nuisance of it is this: that if I say that people should be taught history, I shall have the horrible appearance of presenting myself as a historian. But that is almost the contrary of my contention. I only know a very little history; and even that very little is enough to tell me that much more important and powerful and successful persons than myself know no history at all.

It is not a question of somebody being a scholar; it is a question of something not being taught in the school. If I found that educated people were not aware that there is any difference between addition and subtraction, I should think myself justified in saying that something had happened to arithmetic in the schools; but it would not imply that I am a mathematician, which is absurd; still less that I could discuss the higher mathematics with Professor Einstein. If I found my most cultivated acquaintances alluding to Vienna as the capital of Spain, or the Volga as the chief river of America, I should feel the geographical studies had become a little vague; in spite of the fact that my own knowledge of geography is very vague indeed. In short, an ordinary man is only justified in complaining of the neglect of a subject when he realizes that the schools neglect even the very little that he knows. He may himself have had heavy and laborious difficulties even in mastering the alphabet; but he still has the right to consider it rather odd that people do know the alphabet of arithmetic and do not know the alphabet of history. For the question concerns, in the most emphatic sense, the alphabet of history; the elements of history; or what has been called, in a famous title, the outline of history. I know nothing whatever about electricity, except that it lights bulbs and rings bells, and does all sorts of fantastic things round me, to which I do not happen to attach much importance, as compared with candles or gongs. I know the name comes from the ancient Greek word for amber; but I also know that its modern use has been mainly modern. I mean that, until it was analysed and utilized in the last few centuries by scientific men like Volta or Galvani, few people appreciated the importance of electricity; except those who had the brief but brilliant experience of being struck by lightning. In other words, I mean that, though I know next to nothing about electricity, I know something about the history of electricity, since I know that, before Volta and the rest, it had no history at all.

Now compare that sort of rudimentary information possessed by one ignorant Englishman about a branch of physics with the complete ignorance of almost all Englishmen about a parallel point of history. Millions of men who know much more about electricity than I do (and nobody could know less) are at this moment convinced that internationalism is a new ideal; and that this kind of ethics is as recent as electricity—or, rather, as recent as electricians. Talk to almost anybody in a train or a tram, and you will find he believes that we all emerged out of savage separate tribes, and that the idea of friendship with foreigners is part of a modern ideal of fraternity. Perhaps he will vaguely suppose that the Communists were the first Cosmopolitans; that nothing can link up nations but the Third or Fourth or Fifth or Sixth International, and the alliance of the Proletarians Of All Lands. But that is only a possibility; for the Communists are still a small minority. But even if he is quite a mild and moderate citizen, of the older parties, you will find he believes that national bigotry is merely a thing of the past; or perhaps that international brotherhood can only be a thing of the future. He will say it is due to the growth of liberal ideas, which have widened the narrow sympathies of the nation and the tribe. He may even hold that Mr. Wells invented the World State; even if he has not exactly founded the World State. But, anyhow, he will almost certainly believe, in one way or another, that going back into the past means going back into more and more partisan patches of patriotism; that the world began by being jingo and has gradually grown more sympathetic with justice to the foreigner.

Now, that is a black-and-white blunder about the outline of history; just as it would be a blunder to say that any prehistoric man was an electrician if he was struck by a thunderbolt. It is completely and colossally the contrary of the fact. Europe is now very national, and some may say very narrow. But certainly it was once much less national and much less narrow. Personally, I rather like nationalism; and I know there are much worse things than narrowness. But I am talking about a historical fact, a plain and primary historical fact; a fact that stands in history exactly as addition and subtraction stand in arithmetic. Nobody who does not know it knows the alphabet of our human history. The fact is, of course, that a narrow nationality has grown steadily and strongly for the last six hundred years; and European nations are much more divided now than they were in the time of the Holy Roman Empire, to say nothing of the Pagan Roman Empire. The French and English who fought each other at Crecy were more like each other than the French and English who supported each other at Mons. Our nationalities, whether good or bad (and they are good enough for me) did in historical fact emerge into separate existence out of a common cosmopolitan civilization, dating from the days of the Cæsars, and still recognized in the days of the mediæval Popes. Now, I am not arguing here about what importance is to be attached to this historical fact; still less about what deductions are to be drawn from it. I only say that the fact is not popularly recognized as a fact like the fact of electricity. I only say that I should be universally regarded as an idiot if I were quite so ignorant of electricity as most of my countrymen are of history.

I think it rather important to press the point; because it is at this moment a point of peril. Everybody is asking in a distracted fashion whether the great nations can understand each other; and nearly everybody is insisting that it must be an entirely new sort of understanding. Now, it is surely not unimportant to point out that all these great nations formed part one common and completely united civilization for about sixteen hundred years. I do not want them to fade back into the pagan unity of the first century or the feudal unity of the fourteenth. But if anybody says that they cannot find a unity, it is not irrelevant to say that they did find it, for much more than a thousand years. It is more hopeful to say that international brotherhood was the whole historic background from which we came than to say that it may or may not appear as an untried Utopia.

I READ a chance phrase in a daily paper the other day; indeed, I had read it in a great many other daily papers on a great many other days. But it suddenly revealed to me the deep disagreement that divides most modern people about the nature of progress; even those who are so superficial as to imagine that they all agree. The sentence ran something like this: "The time will come when communicating with the remote stars will seem to us as ordinary as answering the telephone."

To which I answer, by way of a beginning: "Yes, that is what I object to." Now, if you could say to me: "The time will come when answering the telephone will seem to us as extraordinary as communicating with the remote stars . . . ," then I should admit that you were a real, hearty, hopeful, encouraging progressive. Though a progressive, you would still be a prophet; which some have considered to be a rather antiquated trade. It would still be very arguable that a prophet is either a man divinely inspired or a man who, by the nature of the case, is talking about things he does not understand. But, assuming, for the sake of argument, that a progressive can be sufficiently convinced and assured to talk like a prophet, I should say that this prophet was really prophesying the coming of the kingdom of heaven, and this progressive was promising us a real and substantial progress. To tell us that we shall find as much joy in a telephonic voice as we might find in a starry vision —that would be a gospel in the very practical sense of good news. But to tell us that we shall be as much bored by the stars as we are by the telephone—that is not good news at all. It only means that something which is still a sort of vague inspiration will become, in due course, a very ordinary irritation. When the morning stars sing together and the sons of God shout for joy, when the mightiest music of the spheres reaches our earth as a new revelation of the depths and heights of sound, we should not exactly wish that the starry choir should cry in one united chorus: "Sorry you've been troubled." For in that pathetic cry from the exchange, the tragedy of our human lot is philosophically conceded. It is admitted, in the very words, that being called upon to answer the telephone *is* being troubled.

It is admitted, even by the official mind, that in this sense man is born for trouble as the electric sparks fly upward, or wherever the electric sparks may fly; it is even hinted, though perhaps mystically and indirectly, that a life of peace, perfect peace, would be one in which the telephone ceased from troubling and the subscribers were at rest. But the truth goes deeper than any incidental irritations that might arise from the mismanagement of the instrument; it implies some degree of indifference even in the management of it. We are incessantly told, indeed, that the modern scientific appliances, even those like the telephone, which are now universally applied, are the miracles of man, and the marvels of science, and the wonders of the new world. But though the inventions are talked of in this way, they are not treated in this way. Or, rather, if they are so talked of in theory, they are not so talked of in practice. There has certainly been a rush of discovery, a rapid series of inventions; and, in one sense, the activity is marvellous and the rapidity might well look like magic. But it has been a rapidity in things going stale; a rush downhill to the flat and dreary world of the prosaic; a haste of marvellous things to lose their marvellous character; a deluge of wonders to destroy wonder. This may be the improvement of machinery, but it cannot possibly be the improvement of man. And since it is not the improvement of man, it cannot possibly be progress. Man is the creature that progress professes to improve; it is not a race of wheels against wheels, or a wrestling match of engines against engines. Improvement implies all that is commonly called education; and education implies enlargement; and especially enlargement of the imagination.

It implies exactly that imaginative intensity of appreciation which does not permit anything that might be vivid or significant to become trivial or vulgar. If we have vulgarized electricity on the earth, it is no answer to boast that, in a few years more, we can vulgarize the stars in the sky.

Tell me that the bustling business man is struck rigid in prayer at the mere sound of the telephone-bell, like the peasants of Millet at the Angelus; tell me that he bows in reverence as he approaches the shrine of the telephone-box; tell me even that he hails it with Pagan rather than with Christian ritual, that he gives his ear to the receiver as to an Oracle of Delphi, or thinks of the young lady on an office-stool at the Exchange as of a priestess seated upon a tripod in a distant temple; tell me even that he has an ordinary poetical appreciation of the idea of that human voice coming across hills and valleys—as much appreciation as men had about the horn of Roland or the shout of Achilles—tell me that these scenes of adoration or agitation are common in the commercial office on the receipt of a telephone call, and *then* (upon the preliminary presumption that I believe a word you say), *then* indeed I will follow your bustling business man and your bold, scientific inventor to the conquest of new worlds and to the scaling of the stars. For then I shall know that they really do find what they want and understand what they find; I shall know that they do add new experiences to our life and new powers and passions to our souls; that they are like men finding new languages, or new arts, or new schools of architecture. But all they can say, in the sort of passage I quoted, is that they can invent things which are generally commonplace conveniences, but very often commonplace inconveniences. And all that they can boast, in answer to any intelligent criticism, is that they may yet learn how to make the sun and moon and the everlasting heavens equally commonplace, and probably equally inconvenient.

Let it be noted that this is *not,* as is always loosely imagined, a reaction against material science; or a regret for mechanical invention; or a depreciation of telephones or telescopes or anything else. It is exactly the other way. I am not depreciating telephones; I am complaining that they are not appreciated. I am not attacking inventions; I am attacking indifference to inventions. I only remark that it is the same people who brag about them who are really indifferent to them. I am not objecting to the statement that the science of the modern world is wonderful; I am only objecting to the modern world because it does not wonder at it. It is true that, in connexion with certain other political or moral questions, I doubt whether these mechanical tricks can be used as moral tests. But that has nothing to do with the question of the dazzling brilliancy of the conjuring trick, considered as a conjuring trick.

-C 185 ꝛ-

Whether such a thing is an ultimate social test is really a question of whether it is a necessity or a luxury. And nobody ever doubted that a conjuring trick is a luxury. The ideal of a peasantry, enunciated by a French king, that there should always be a chicken in the pot, is doubtless different from the ideal that there should always be a rabbit in the hat. But there is no reason to doubt that the French king and the French peasant are capable of enjoying the purely artistic and scientific pleasure of seeing the rabbit rapidly and dexterously produced from the hat. Now I may, and do, doubt whether there is very much purely *practical* superiority in the extraordinary rabbit over the ordinary chicken. I doubt whether great masses of men will get much more food off the magical rabbit than greyhounds will get off the mechanical hare. I doubt whether rabbit tastes any nicer out of the hat of a professor in evening dress than out of the pot of a French peasant's wife who happens to know how to cook it. In short, my doubts about modern materialistic machinery are doubts about its ultimate utility in practice. But I never questioned its poetry, its fantasy; the fitness of so sublime a conjuring trick for a children's party. What I complain of is that the modern children have forgotten how to shriek.

THE time has come to protest against certain very grave perils in the cinema and the popular films. I do not mean the peril of immoral films, but the peril of moral ones. I have, indeed, a definite objection to immoral films, but it is becoming more and more difficult to discuss a definite morality with people whose very immorality is indefinite. And, for the rest, merely lowbrow films seem to me much more moral than many of the highbrow ones. Mere slapstick pantomime, farces of comic collapse and social topsy-turvydom, are, if anything, definitely good for the soul. To see a banker or broker or prosperous business man running after his hat, kicked out of his house, hurled from the top of a skyscraper, hung by one leg to an aeroplane, put into a mangle, rolled out flat by a steam-roller, or suffering any such changes of fortune, tends in itself rather to edification; to a sense of the insecurity of earthly things and the folly of that pride which is based on the accident of prosperity. But the films of which I complain are not those in which famous or fashionable persons become funny or undignified, but those in which they become far too dignified and only unintentionally funny.

In this connexion, it is especially the educational film that threatens to darken and weaken the human intelligence. I do not mean the educational film in the technical or scientific sense; the presentation of the definite details of some science or branch of study. In these innocent matters, even education can do comparatively little harm to the human brain. There are a number of really delightful films, for instance, dealing with exploration and local aspects of biology or botany. Nothing could be more charmingly fanciful than such natural history; especially when its monsters seem to emulate the Snark or the Jumblies, and become figures of unnatural history. But in that sort of unnatural history there is nothing unnatural. The Loves of the Penguins are doubtless as pure as the Loves of the Triangles; and to see a really fine film in which an elephant playfully smashes up four or five flourishing industrial towns or imperial outposts only realizes a daydream already dear to every healthy human instinct. Where the real peril begins to appear is not in natural history, but in history. It is in the story of those talkative and inventive penguins of whom M. Anatole France wrote in the tale of that terrible and incalculable creature, who is so much more ruthless and devastating than the wildest rogue elephant, since he does not destroy industrial cities, but builds them.

In short, it is in relation with the story of Man, the monster of all monsters and the mystery of all mysteries, that our natural history may become in the dangerous sense unnatural. And everybody knows that the commonest way in which history can grow crooked, or become unnatural, is through partisanship and prejudice, and the desire to draw too simple a moral from only one side of the case. Now, it is just here that the most successful films are in some danger of becoming actually anti-educational, while largely professing to be educational. In this connexion, it will be well to recall two or three determining facts of the general situation of society and the arts to-day. The first fact to realize is this: that only a little while ago the more thick-headed prejudices of provincial history were beginning to wear a little thin. Men would still take, as they were entitled to take, their own side according to their own sympathies. But they were beginning to realize that history consists of human beings, and not of heroes and villains out of an old Adelphi melodrama. Whether men were for or against Queen Elizabeth, they did begin to understand that she was something a little more complex than Good Queen Bess; and that even her unfortunate sister was in a situation not to be completely simplified by the use of a popular expletive, as in Bloody Mary.

It began to be admitted that the great seventeenth-century struggle, about whether England should be a Monarchy or an Aristocracy, could not be used merely to prove that Cromwell was never anything but a saint or Charles I never anything but a martyr. This great change for the good was very largely connected with the passing of the old Two-Party System. There had been a time when people were told to choose, not so much between Gladstone and Disraeli, as between a popular figure who was not Gladstone and another popular figure who was not Disraeli. The wary Old Parliamentary Hand, with his Tory traditions of the Oxford Movement, was represented as a wild, revolutionary idealist, everywhere demanding that the heavens should fall, that some Utopian justice might be done. The cynical cosmopolitan adventurer, with his romantic loyalty to Israel and his open contempt for the common Conservative point of view, was praised as a hearty English country gentleman, innocently interested in crops which consisted chiefly of primroses. These fatuous electioneering fictions were beginning to fade away; partly through a reaction towards the rather acid Lytton Strachey biographies, partly through a more sane and liberal historical interest in historical characters who really were very interesting human beings. And then, when the truth was beginning to pierce through in books, and even in newspapers, the whole light was blotted out by a big, fashionable film, cunningly written and brilliantly performed, in which Disraeli appeared once

more as God's Englishman covered with primroses
and breathing the innocent patriotism of our native
fields.

The second fact to remember is a certain privi-
lege almost analogous to monopoly, which belongs
of necessity to things like the theatre and the
cinema. In a sense more than the metaphorical,
they fill the stage; they dominate the scene; they
create the landscape. That is why one need not
be Puritanical to insist on a somewhat stricter
responsibility in all sorts of play-acting than in
the looser and less graphic matter of literature.
If a man is repelled by one book, he can shut it
and open another; but he cannot shut up a theatre
in which he finds a show repulsive, nor instantly
order one of a thousand other theatres to suit his
taste. There are a limited number of theatres; and
even to cinemas there is some limit. Hence there
is a real danger of historical falsehood being
popularized through the film, because there is not
the normal chance of one film being corrected by
another film. When a book appears displaying a
doubtful portrait of Queen Elizabeth, it will
generally be found that about six other historical
students are moved to publish about six other
versions of Queen Elizabeth at the same moment.
We can buy Mr. Belloc's book on Cromwell, and
then Mr. Buchan's book on Cromwell; and pay our
money and take our choice. But few of us are in
a position to pay the money required to stage a

complete and elaborately presented alternative film-version of Disraeli. The fiction on the film, the partisan version in the movie-play, will go uncontradicted and even uncriticized, in a way in which few provocative books can really go uncontradicted and uncriticized. There will be no opportunity of meeting it on its own large battle-field of expansive scenario and multitudinous repetition. And most of those who are affected by it will know or care very little about its being brought to book by other critics and critical methods. The very phrase I have casually used, "brought to book," illustrates the point. A false film might be refuted in a hundred books, without much affecting the million dupes who had never read the books but only seen the film. The protest is worth making, because provincial prejudice of this kind is frightfully dangerous in the present international problem of the hour. It is perfectly natural for nations to have a patriotic art, and even within reason a patriotic education. It naturally teaches people, especially young people, to be proud of the great heroes of their great history; and to conceive their own past in a sort of poetic way like legends. But this is exactly where we may test the difference between a legend and a lie. The outlines of a real hero, like Nelson or Sarsfield, are not altered when the figure is filled up, in maturer stages of knowledge, by the facts about failure or weakness or limitation. The hero remains a hero; though the child, being now grown up, knows that a hero is a man. But the figure of the fictitious Beaconsfield will not support the intrusion of the real Disraeli. It would be destroyed by all that was most interesting in Disraeli; even by all that was most genuine in Disraeli. A dummy of that sort does no good to national credit or glory; all foreigners laugh at it, knowing more about it than we do; and we ourselves can only preserve our solemnity by not going near enough to laugh. That is to make the thing a mere "film" on the eyes of official obscurantism; and to give a new secretive meaning to the title of "The Screen."

WHATEVER else was evolved, evolution was not
evolved. I mean evolution as a part of education; as an idea more or less accepted for the
last forty years by most thinking people; and
perhaps even more by most unthinking people.
Those who supported it were always talking about
growth and gradual change; but their own movement was not at all gradual. They popularized an
evolution that was far too much of a revolution;
that came with far too much of a rush; that became
as the phrase goes, all the rage; with some of its
exponents rather unmistakably raging. It was
opposed to ideas of supernatural or even special
creation; but the theory itself was created in a very
special sense; and it was boomed and advertised
like a miracle. Many of the recent revolts and
reactions and belated questionings have been due
to that original journalistic hustle; and yet they
are themselves likely to be treated in turn in too
hustling and journalistic a fashion. Darwin's
individual industry was indeed minute and patient;
and he was personally the very reverse of an
impetuous or impatient character. It is none the
less true that Darwinism was much too hastily

thrust down everybody's throat, including Darwin's. Old Huxley had all the passions of a pamphleteer and a partisan; also he was individually and intensely interested in certain ethical and philosophical attitudes of his own, which Darwinism supported more perhaps than he himself would otherwise have supported Darwinism. Huxley and Herbert Spencer really valued Darwinism, as an argument for agnosticism. It would have been much better if they had cultivated a little more agnosticism about Darwinism.

All the memoirs and memories of that time are full of that curious atmosphere of brand-new prejudice and premature pugnacity. Popular science loved to put the spotlight on special occasions; party combats and particular challenges of particular champions. Everybody talked about the repartee of Huxley to Wilberforce as something as theatrical as a thunderbolt. Everything was supposed to stand or fall by a particular debate between Huxley and Gladstone about the Gadarene Swine. Nobody seems to have remarked on the fact that a theory like Darwinism, advanced by a man like Darwin, was about the most unsuitable subject on earth to be settled by a retort in a debating club. Nobody noticed that Gladstone was about the worst person in the world either to teach a man like Huxley the truths of theology or to detect in him the errors of science. Humanity knew that Gladstone was an eloquent orator, and

Huxley said he was a copious shuffler; but he was neither a philosopher nor a historian suited to deal with the theory of evidence of miracles. He was simply the Prime Minister, past, present, or to come; and his appearance on that platform only made it a fashionable occasion. That was what was the matter with the whole occasion. Darwin became much too fashionable; and Darwinism prevailed only as a fashion.

If the great biological speculations of the later nineteenth century had remained speculative, they would have been much more slow and very much more sure. We might by this time have really taken stock of what is actually known about the variation of species and what can only be plausibly guessed and what is quite random guesswork. Instead of that, a hypothesis was allowed to harden into a habit of thought; and any alternative hypothesis creates unnecessary excitement as a violent paradox. A distinguished scientific man, in another branch of science, has recently contradicted Darwinism with the same emphasis and eagerness with which the Darwinians affirmed it. This is news in the newspapers, but in this country we grossly exaggerate the extent to which it is new in the scientific world. When Sir Arthur Keith and Mr. H. G. Wells tried to treat Anti-Darwinism as an unheard-of paradox, Mr. Belloc had not the least difficulty in naming fifty scientific men of the first rank, throughout Europe, who were avowed

Anti-Darwinians. And Sir Arthur Keith could say nothing in reply, except that one out of the fifty, the distinguished Professor Dwight, had never at any time accepted the Darwinian hypothesis. The argument was, apparently, that Dwight could not be right, because he had been right all the time. There is nothing new about the purely scientific attack on the Darwinian theory; it began very soon after the Darwinians advanced the theory. But the Darwinians advanced it with so sweeping and hasty an intolerance that it is no longer a question of one scientific theory being advanced against another scientific theory. It is no longer a question of fairly comparing what Darwin said with what Dwight said; indeed, it is not a question at all. It is treated as an answer; and a final and infallible answer. Now nobody need know any more than the mere rudiments of the biological controversy in order to know that, touching twenty incidental problems, it is in some ways a very unsatisfactory answer. This does not necessarily mean that it was not valuable as a suggestion; or that it may not help to suggest the real answer. Darwin did a mass of very fine work, accummulated a multitude of facts, and set them in a certain light by subjecting them to a general suggestion. Such work need not have been thrown away if the thing had been treated in a reasonable manner. The Victorian evolutionists were wrong; not because they opened the evolutionary question, but because they closed it.

For the Victorian evolutionists were very Victorian indeed. They really did deserve the sort of criticism which the realists of a younger generation have brought against Victorian virtue or hypocrisy, in the matter of closed doors. Yet the evil did not really come from hypocrisy; it did really come from virtue. But it was virtue of a certain Puritanical type; and especially of a political type. The men of whom Thomas Huxley was the greatest were, above all, controversialists; because they were, above all, moralists. They conducted their debates, even their abstract scientific debates, in the spirit of a sort of idealistic General Election. It was Darwin against Gladstone; just as it was Disraeli against Gladstone. They were always going to the country, appealing to the public, expecting an immediate decision of the whole commonwealth, even on the most specialist speculations, as if they were the most spiritual elements of right and wrong. Thus they identified Free Trade with Freedom; insisting on it with an ethical simplicity wholly inapplicable to an economic science. And so they identified Natural Selection with Nature; with a dogmatic finality wholly inapplicable to a biological science. The Darwinian Theory was the Dawn; and any other shade of fact or fancy was only part of the opposing darkness. We can see the difference in a flash if we merely compare those great and grim grey-whiskered men with the Greeks or the men of the Renaissance, when they speculated in a free-and-easy fashion about some theory of the stars, or the flight of birds, or the movements of the sea. The greater moral seriousness of the Victorians gave them all the advantage that industry and conscientious record can give; but there is a sense in which the scientific spirit was lost in the very triumphs of the scientific age. They were so fond of having convictions that they came prematurely to conclusions. Having grown doubtful about the things on which conviction is most valuable, they then expected the speculative imagination to answer as promptly and practically as the conscience. The consequence was that they answered much too soon; and then yielded to the temptation of all moralists, to veto any kind of answer to the answer. Anyone who reads the account of how the orthodox officials of Darwinism dealt with a real free-thinker like Samuel Butler will recognize by unmistakable signs that the Darwinian free-thinkers were no longer thinking freely; we might say they were no longer free to think. The consequence is that, by this time, when that rigid and respectable Victorian front door is suddenly burst open, it has the effect of a resurrection or the rending of a tomb. But there is no need for such excitement; and it is quite possible that the reaction following such a resurrection may go too far. It will be worse still if the world is again converted without being convinced.

It is well that students sternly devoted to that science should issue bulletins, from time to time, upon the state of the Detective Story; the stage it has recently reached in its present alleged progress or decline. Some hold that the possibilities of the detective story will soon be exhausted. They take the view that there are only a limited number of ways of murdering a man, or only a limited number of men who might plausibly and reasonably be murdered. But surely this is to take too gloomy and pessimistic a view of the case. Some hold that the detective story will, indeed, progress and evolve, but it will evolve into something else; and I always think that sort of evolution is a form of extinction. They seem to think that it will become so good that it will cease to exist; will die of sheer goodness, like the little choir-boy. What used to be called the police novel will expand into the novel where the problems are too subtle to be solved by calling in the police. For my part, as a matter of taste, I can do very well without the police; but I cannot do without the criminals. And if modern writers are going to ignore the existence of crime, as so many of them already ignore

the existence of sin, then modern writing will get
duller than ever.

Here, however, my only duty, as a dry recorder
of scientific facts, is to note a few of the recent
changes in the police novel, which do roughly
correspond to changes in the social history of our
time. I shall also venture, in my capacity of earnest
ethical adviser to the young student of blood and
thunder, to point out some dangers and disadvan-
tages in these new forms and fashions in crime.
For, though modern society has given us in some
ways a wider range, and provided us with varieties
of incident or implement not known to our fathers
and mothers, and all the other simple and homely
assassins of our childhood's days, yet this enlargement and variety is not an unmixed advantage for
the artist in murder. There are several ways, in this
as in other arts of life, in which the modern appearance of liberty is very misleading. Many a
happy family, innocently priding itself on an uncle
who was hanged in the quiet old Victorian days,
would, in fact, find that their relative's career made
a much better story, considered as a story, than
some of these larger and looser studies of loose living, where there are so many new vices to cover the
track of ancient crime.

I would therefore lay down this canon first of
all: that the people in a really gory murder mystery
should be good people. Even the man who is really
gory should be good, or should have a convincing

appearance of being good. Now, many of the very best of the modern writers in this style have partly failed through neglecting this maxim. They start out with another maxim, which is also in itself a perfectly sound maxim. They start out with the very reasonable idea of giving the reader a wide choice of suspects, that the imagination may hover long over them all before it swoops (if it ever does swoop) upon the really guilty person. Unfortunately, it is exactly here that the laxity of modern manners, not to say morals, actually comes in to spoil the effect. The writer begins with somebody doing what (I believe) is known as throwing a party; as a preliminary to the more private act of throwing another party, in the sense of another person, out of a window or down a well. The whole business begins in a rather heated atmosphere of cocktails, with occasional whiffs of cocaine. And the charming freedom and variety of such a social set, in these days, enables the author to crowd the room with all sorts of people who, in the older story, could only have escaped from Dartmoor or returned by ticket-of-leave from Botany Bay. The chief ornaments of these aristocratic salons are conspicuous, not merely by being cads, but by having every appearance of being criminals. In short, the suspects are so very suspect that we might safely call them guilty; not necessarily of the crime under discussion, but only of about half a hundred others.

But there is an obvious snag in this convenient way of spreading suspicion over a number of characters. It can be put in a word: such cases may cause suspicion, but they cannot cause surprise. It is the business of a shocker to produce a shock. But these modern characters are much too shocking ever to produce a shock. These dubious dopers, these suspected dope-traffickers, these alleged or half-alleged heroes of horrible scandals in the past—all these livers of the wild life have one inevitable touch of tameness. They all have one element that must make any ending of the story tame. And that is, that no reader would be even mildly astonished to learn that any one of them, or all of them, had committed the crime. It is true that, in some of the very best recent *romans policiers,* this rout of rather bestial revellers is often introduced, not in order to convict any of them, but to distract attention from some seemingly conventional person who is ultimately convicted. But the method is wrong, even at the best; a hint of guilt should be thrilling; but there is nothing particularly thrilling about the safe bet that some of these social ornaments are capable of being thieves or thugs. If what we want is a thrill, the thrill could only be found in the virtuous Victorian household, when it was first realized that Grandmama's throat had been cut by the curate or by the rather too well-behaved nursery-governess. Even the love of murder stories, like other moral and religious tendencies, will lead us back to home and the simple life.

I think there is another weak point, which is the worst thing even in the best shockers. This also is connected with some recent social changes; as with the scientific fashion of Psychoanalysis, which is generally more of a fashion than a science. It is also connected with a certain mechanical or materialistic interpretation of human interests, which often goes along with it. I mean the expedient of distracting attention from the real criminal by suspecting him at the beginning and not merely at the end. It generally takes the form of some apparent conviction or confession, first dismissed as impossible, and finally found, by some unsuspected ingenuity, to have been possible after all. Often the first accusation is dismissed by some of the dogmas of the new psychology. The curate, let us say, confesses that he jumped over an incredibly high wall to murder the grandmother; and the professor of psychology (with the piercing eyes) points out that a theological training had repressed instead of liberated the *libido* of the curate in the direction of trespass and burglary. He had dreamed he jumped over a high wall; or perhaps the height symbolized levitation and ascending into heaven; it is an accommodating science. Then when we think that the curate is cleared and out of it, we are relieved to find in the last chapter that he is the criminal after all; both he and the author having concealed up to this moment the fact that the curate held the International Championship for the High Jump, and had concealed a jumping-pole among the poles used for the punt.

This method, again, has every quality of ingenuity, and pursues the highly legitimate aim of shifting the spot light from the guilty to the innocent. And yet I think that it fails, and that there is a reason for its failure. The error is the materialistic error; the mistake of supposing that our interest in the plot is mechanical, when it is really moral. But art is never unmoral, though it is sometimes immoral; that is, moral with the wrong morality. The only thrill, even of a common thriller, is concerned somehow with the conscience and the will; it involves finding out that men are worse or better than they seem, and that by their own choice. Therefore, there can never be quite so much excitement over the mere mechanical truth of how a man managed to do something difficult as over the mere fact that he wanted to do it. In these cases we have already considered the criminal as a criminal; we are only asked to consider him anew as a cracksman or crafty and clever criminal. The effect of this is always a sort of bathos; an anti-climax. I say it with regret, for it figures in some of the finest mystery stories I know. But, even if the book is of the best, it always makes me feel that the last page is the worst; when the last page should be the best of all.

I notice a curiously modern and sullen realism beginning to settle on some of the recognized tales of murder, once so gay, innocent, and refreshing. Once our detective art really was almost an unmoral art; and therefore the one which managed to remain almost a moral art. But shades of the prison-house—or, worse still, of the humane reformatory and the psychological clinic—begin to close upon the growing boy and the hopeful butcher of his kind. We are given detailed descriptions of depressing domestic interiors, as if being dumbly asked whether a wife so involved in the washing or the dusting or the spring-cleaning was not eventually bound to murder or be murdered in any case. It is all very well, but I would point out to the sanguinary sophist that the argument can be turned the other way. If it be true that a misguided wife may begin thoughtlessly by doing the washing, and find all sorts of vexatious consequences, possibly including death by violence, so it is equally true that she may begin by using murder as a minor gadget in the domestic machinery, taking death by violence in her stride as a plain, practical solution; and then, after all, find herself involved in a most inordinate amount of washing.

There could not be a grimmer example of this tragedy than poor Lady Macbeth. She had her faults, perhaps, but there is no ground for accusing her of any rooted or aboriginal taste for hygiene. When she was young and innocent, her imagination seems to have been quite unpolluted by the impure image of soap. I should even hesitate to accuse her of spring-cleaning in the serious, anti-social, and sinful sense of the term. Anyhow, a number of very different birds seem to have nested undisturbed over the main entrance to the reception-rooms; which looks as if she was once a human being, and more interested in spring-broods than in spring-cleaning. Unfortunately, like such a very large number of people living in dark, barbarous, ignorant, and ferocious times, she was full of modern ideas. She intended especially to maintain the two brightest and most philosophical of modern ideas; first, that it is often extremely convenient to do what is wrong; and second, that whenever it is convenient to do what is wrong, it immediately becomes what is right. Illuminated by these two scientific searchlights of the twentieth century in her groping among the stark trees and stone pillars of the Dark Ages, Lady Macbeth thought it quite simple and business-like to kill an old gentleman of very little survival value, and offer her own talents to the world in the capacity of Queen. It seems natural enough; to most of us who are used to the morals of modern novels, it will seem almost humdrum and tiresomely obvious. And yet see what a snag there was in it after all!

On this one doomed and devoted woman, who

had done nothing but a little bit of a murder which she thought little enough of at the time (as De Quincey says), there fell from heaven like the Deluge the deathly curse of Cleanliness. She, who seems never to have known such morbidities before, was tortured with horrid suggestions of washing her hands, and pursued by furies who seem to have taken the form of modern salesmen offering different brands of soap. Those ambitions of the house-wife, which seem to the modern moralist so obvious a cause of murder, were, in fact, wildly exaggerated in her case as a consequence of murder. It was the worst doom of the murderess that she wanted to do the washing, not on Monday, but at midnight; that she wanted to have a spring-cleaning, not in the spring of the year, but in the middle of the night. Who shall say lightly that a murder or two does not matter, when it may lead to the murderess becoming as hygienic as all that?

Sinister minds may be clouded by dark and unworthy suspicions that the views here discussed are not wholly serious; but some of the modern moralists favouring murder and other simple solutions of social difficulties are serious with a dry-throated earnestness that no satire could simulate. And even my own lighted prejudices on the negative side are not without spasms of sincerity. I certainly do not like that Religion of Ablutions which has always really been the Religion of Pharisees; even when it masqueraded as the

Religion of Anglo-Saxons or the Religion of Muscular Christians. I made fun of it when it was blindly worshipped, though I have lived to see it too blindly and sweepingly derided, as the Religion of Pukka Sahibs or the Religion of Public School Men. And I know that in its domestic form it can sometimes produce a Puritanism that is very close indeed to Pharisaism. But I should still regard it rather as a symptom of social evil than as a necessary cause of social crime. Miss Miggs will sometimes make almost as much fuss about a spot of grease as Lady Macbeth about a spot of blood. But to infer from this that we are bound to murder Miss Miggs, and that Lady Macbeth was bound to murder Duncan, and that everybody is bound to murder everybody whom he happens to find troublesome for any reason for any considerable length of time—that is one of the dubious and creeping deductions which are beginning to appear, more or less tentatively, in many of the tragedies published in our time; and I should like to protest against all such savage fatalism, before it becomes more explicit. It is, of course, only the logical consequence, as applied to the problem of murder, of what is now everywhere applied to the problem of marriage. It is the theory that there is no such thing as an intolerable solution of a problem, but only an intolerable acceptance of a problem. It is the theory that nothing can possibly be unendurable except having to endure. It is interesting to see how rapidly and quietly the same ethical spirit is already beginning to work in other fields of thought. It does really seem to me far less fantastic to say that a mania for washing was a mild and merciful punishment for murder than to say that murder is a just and reasonable punishment for a mania for washing. But, in any case, I protest against that arbitrary gesture of self-ablution and self-absolution with which some characters in modern stories conclude the confession of their crimes; like that weak tyrant who tried to combine the contraries of despotism and irresponsibility by washing his hands when he had delivered the innocent to death.

It amuses me to think that, amid all the invocations of Christmas and invocations to Christmas
charity, I am probably in a minority in uttering
any particular and positive eulogy of Christmas
waits. It is common enough to celebrate the jovial
season by making jokes about Christmas waits,
but they are generally in the same vein as the jokes
about Christmas bills. It is constantly said in the
newspapers (and therefore it must be true) that
we have everywhere increased in social sympathies
and sentiments of human brotherhood, and it is
sometimes even said that all classes are drawing
together in mutual understanding. I am sure I
hope it may be so; and indeed I think that in
certain special social aspects it is so. But I notice
that, in many houses where a previous generation
accepted waits and carol-singers, even if they
grumbled at them in secret, with all the external
courtesy and resignation of Duke Theseus listening
to the play of Pyramus and Thisbe in *A Midsummer
Night's Dream,* many of a later generation have
grown less patient and less polite. I also notice
that, over vast districts of the modern urban civilization, whole streets are plastered with placards

forbidding hawkers and street cries; lest the ancient institution of the pedlar or the last of the old music of London should disturb those within who are intently occupied, let us hope, in studying books on evolutionary ethics by Cambridge economists, which demonstrate so radiantly the need of social contacts and the removal of all barriers between class and class. Having read a vast number of books of that sort in my time, I am still not entirely satisfied that, in every respect, they are invariably more human and amusing than the talk of Autolycus or the tune of "Cherry-Ripe."

But there is a special case for carol-singers, because they come at a time when our whole tradition has always told us to be charitable to strangers, even to beggars. Of course, carol-singers are not in any sense whatever beggars. They are people offering something in return for money; we may not happen to think it is worth the money, and I happen to think exactly the same of about three-quarters of the things that are most boomed and pushed in the modern business market. But in so far as many of us do pay for the entertainment, even when we do not particularly want the entertainment, and do it from motives of charity, the waits or carol-singers can in that sense be put into the same class as beggars, and sink instantly to the abject and degraded condition of Homer or St. Francis of Assisi. And it is about this problem of beggars, or of those who in one aspect are in the position of beggars, that I am disposed to raise a very general question and remark on a general comparison.

I happen myself to represent, more or less, a general moral philosophy which until very lately was the general moral philosophy of most nations and even most confessions in Europe. And in nothing was that general tradition of our fathers more criticized by our contemporaries than in its alleged contentment with casual and sporadic charity; or, in other words, the habit of giving money to beggars. Now, there is a rather interesting parallel here, between the nineteenth-century attitude towards the problem of the beggar and the twentieth-century attitude towards the problem of the soldier. Only too often, and to the deep disgrace of governments, they were the same individuals. There was a beggars' rhyme in my boyhood that ran: "Here comes a poor soldier from Botany Bay; What have you got to give him to-day?" In the eyes of many modern scientific humanitarians and philanthropists (who certainly would have nothing to give him), he would be blasted with a sort of series and crescendo of crimes; horrible because he was a beggar; horrible because he was a convict, from Botany Bay or any other convict settlement; and most horrible of all because he was a soldier. But both in his character of a beggar and his character of a soldier he offers an opportunity for explaining a certain old-fashioned point of view, which I fancy the majority of modern people do not understand at all.

Those modern people who, much more than any ancient people, have refused and repulsed beggars as such were not merely brutal or stingy. The thing was perhaps at its worst in the blackest time of industrial individualism, when even the theories were brutal and stingy; we might almost say, in some cases, that the ideals were brutal and stingy. But this would be unjust to a very large number of the theorists and idealists who really did believe in plausible theories and ideals. The first theory that held the field was something like this: that it was uneconomic and therefore unethical to patch up the position of people who were in the wrong position and even in the wrong place. The theory was that such a person could eventually find his place when the whole economic community could find its level, and each person was achieving the cheapest production at the proper profit or price. The ideal, however vague, was that of a community in which everybody was living productively and profitably, and nobody was living unproductively and unprofitably. Given that ideal, or any real belief in that ideal, it is not difficult to see that the beggar appears an anomaly that ought to disappear. Unfortunately, the ideal has disappeared and the beggar has remained. Nobody now believes that mere individualism and competition will ever, of themselves, work out to that economic paradise of give and take. The death of that delusion was hastened by the Socialists. And whatever be wrong with Socialism, it was entirely right about what is wrong with Individualism. But the Socialist, quite as much as the Individualist, necessarily and naturally regarded the beggar as an anomaly to be abolished. His way of abolishing him was to plan out a series of Utopias in which the State would find everybody the best work and pay everybody the best wages. I am not criticizing those Utopias just now, or rather I am only criticizing them on one small point. So far as this argument goes there is nothing against them, except that they have not happened. Even among the Bolshevists, where something happened, it was not the abolition of beggary, whether this was the fault of the Bolshevists or no. A rich man in the Ukraine famine would be faced with just the same problem of beggars as a rich man in the Irish famine. Now, when one theory after another thus rises and falls, and one Utopian promise after another is made and broken, is it not comprehensible that some of us think it well to save even a solitary man from starvation, while the world is making up its mind how many centuries it will take for starvation to disappear?

As I have hinted, there is something of the same notion in tolerating the soldier as in tolerating the beggar. Nobody wants anybody to beg or anybody to fight. But when promise after promise of universal peace is broken, and conference after conference abandons the task of establishing international justice, is it so very odd that some people should still want something to defend national justice, in the sense of justice to their own nation? And if the beggar and the soldier seem to remain, *since* they seem to remain—then I do most strongly feel that it is better that they should not be regarded merely as blots or pests, but rather in the light of the traditional virtues associated with the tragedy; the one in the light of charity and the other of chivalry. I do not expect every one, or possibly even any one, to agree entirely with this view, but I hope that somebody will at least accept the compromise in the case of Carol-Singers or Waits.

THE world has not yet had the happiness of reading my great forthcoming work, *The Case for
Human Sacrifice, or Moloch the Modern World's
Hope,* in nine volumes, with plates and diagrams
illustrating all the advantages of Ritual Murder,
and the religious side of cannibalism. It is even
possible, alas! that the reader will never have the
rapture of reading this great scientific monograph;
for I have a great many other jobs on hand, in the
distraction and excitement of which it is possible
that my first fiery and youthful enthusiasm for
Human Sacrifice may have somewhat faded, with
the passage of years and the consolidation of more
moderate convictions. But though I doubt whether
I could, by this time, bring myself to sacrifice a
baby to Moloch, and though my first boyish
impatience at the tame compromise adopted in the
cases of Isaac and Iphigenia has long died away, I
still think Human Sacrifice is infinitely more decent
and dignified than some scientific operations proposed at the present time. At least Human Sacrifice
is human; a great deal more human than humanitarianism. And when modern medical men gravely
get up and propose that human beings should be put

in lethal chambers, when there is any reason to fancy that they are tired of life, I am still (relatively) prepared to cry: "Give me Moloch and the cannibals."

First consider the fundamental point: that the pagan altar at least treated a man's life as something valuable, while the lethal chamber treats a man's life as something valueless. A man's life was offered to the gods because it was valuable; more valuable than the best bull or the finest ram, or the choice things from the flocks and herds which were always chosen because they were choice. But the moderns, who do not believe in the existence of gods, tend at last not to believe even in the existence of men. Being scientific evolutionists, they cannot tell the difference between a man and a sheep. And being highly civilized townsmen, they would probably be very bad judges of the difference between a good sheep and a bad one. Therefore, there is in their sacrificial operations a sort of scornful and indifferent quality contrary to the idea of sacrifice, even at its blackest and bloodiest. They are always talking about eliminating the unfit, getting rid of the surplus population, segregating the feeble-minded, or destroying the hopeless; and this gives all their work a character of contempt. Now, in the very vilest blood-rites of barbarians, there may have been cruelty, but there was not contempt. To have your throat cut before an ugly stone idol was a compliment; though perhaps a compliment that you would have politely disclaimed and waved away.

It would have implied that you were, in the words of the old feudal custom of rent, the Best Beast. And however beastly you might think the people around you, and their religious views and liturgical habits, there would be some satisfaction in being the best beast among them. Human Sacrifice had this great though fallen splendour clinging about it; that at least it was the very contrary of the Survival of the Fittest. Like all the deaths of the martyrs and the heroes, it was the Surrender of the Fittest. The scientific destroyers necessarily talk in the opposite terms and spread the opposite tone. They sacrifice the black sheep of the flock; the mad bull of the herd; the unfortunates of the human community whom they choose to regard as mad or merely as weak-minded. They do not merely kill, but annihilate; not only in the sense of reducing people to nothing, but even of regarding them as nobodies. The sacrificial victim was always regarded as something; he was even respected as somebody. The victim was often a princess whose beauty was admired, or a great enemy whose courage was envied. Some have said that the latter was the origin of cannibalism; in which case it would be quite a handsome compliment to be cooked and eaten; and something of a snub or sneer, to any sensitively constituted gentleman, to be spared and left alive. The reader may be relieved to learn, however, that I do not really recommend the inclusion of cannibalism and human sacrifice among the ritualistic innovations of the Advanced School in the Church.

The truth remains, however, even in the literal and Latin meaning of sacrifice. It means to make a thing sacred; or, in this case, to make a man sacred. And to make him sacred is to make him separate; something set apart, and not to be confused with flocks and herds and the beasts that perish. Now the opposite evil, as it exists in so much scientific philanthropy, is the tendency to deal with men in herds; to treat them like sheep; and not only to class them with the beasts that perish but to take particular care that they do perish. And this is tyranny of a new kind, as compared even with the old despotic execution, let alone the old hieratic sacrifice. Even the public executions, now conventionally condemned, had this sort of wild justice about them: that they did not deprive the chief actor of the limelight. But the new death-ray of scientific destruction would not pick out personalities and individuals as does the limelight. And there is danger that the very fact of dealing with lives that are supposed to be futile or featureless or merely uncomfortable and unpleasant, instead of with great crimes or blasphemies, may bring into the business a spirit which is worse than merely cruel; because it is merely callous.

It is a favourite joke among the more solemn historians that Robespierre, credited or discredited with the guillotining of thousands of enemies of his own theory, actually began his political life with an argument for the abolition of Capital Punishment. It is less often noticed, though it is really a better joke, that he used the only really good argument for the abolition of Capital Punishment. He said: "Every time you kill a man by law, you diminish something of the sacredness of Man." But human sacrifice, whatever its other little weaknesses, did not diminish anything of the sacredness of Man. From the point of view of that particular pagan heresy, it even increased the sacredness of Man. For it was founded on the opposite principle, that the best thing must be sacrificed or made sacred. And though this particular form of the sentiment is barbarous and benighted, and in moral practice abominable, the sentiment itself is one which ought to be understood better than it is in what is commonly called an age of enlightenment. Unfortunately, the enlightened are also benighted. They never seem to throw any light on these most mysterious and interesting parts of the nature and history of Man; and since they cannot understand the idea in its highest and purest manifestations, it is natural that they should be merely puzzled by it in its basest and most brutal. But a huge part of human history will remain permanently unintelligible to those who cannot even entertain this idea: the idea of giving up a thing not because it is bad, but because it is good.

Speaking seriously, of course, most human sacrifice tends to be inhuman, because it tends to be diabolist. The line is not always drawn at first, or drawn easily, between a somewhat dark and ruthless deity and an actual demon. But one thing at least we may learn from the real history of the world, and that is how to avoid a blunder made by more than half the histories in the world. Whatever else is true, it is not true that blood-rites belong entirely to prehistoric or even primitive peoples. The progressive historians, of a school no longer very obviously progressing, did their very best to hint and imply that complex civilization is a complete safeguard against unnatural creeds or cruel ceremonies. It is nothing of the kind. Some of the most civilized and highly organized cultures, like Carthage at its wealthiest, had human sacrifice at its worst. Culture, like science, is no protection against demons. And poor Robespierre was nearer the truth than the later progressives when he said that there was no protection for the commonwealth but Virtue and the Worship of God.

I MAY explain that I am one of the people who really like weddings. Or, rather, to speak more strictly, I am one of the few people who admit, and even boast, that they like weddings. If I took quite simply and seriously the testimony of a long succession of individuals whom I have met, and with whom I have conversed on the topic, I should be bound to deduce that they all of them detest weddings. They always describe them as orgies of futility and fatigue; as occasions of flaunting vulgarity or sickly sentimentalism; as crushes and crowds of stuffy relations, made more insupportable by the intolerable presence of priests or parsons in churches or chapels; for it is generally agreed that having to have parsons is an even more horrible calamity than the horror of having any relations. In short, it may logically and definitely be deduced that most human beings abhor and repudiate weddings, especially these important weddings; which is why the church is always crowded to the roof with a mob big enough to burst all the doors and windows.

In fact, I have noticed that the person who claims to hate weddings is generally the person who makes them hateful. It is precisely the sort of lady who stands on a chair to count the duchesses, or talks in a loud voice about who might have married whom, who eventually staggers out of the crowd, laden with snapshots of all the wealthiest people and autographs of all the more vulgar celebrities, to cry aloud in utter weariness how much she loathes weddings. But all these loathsome things, including the lady herself, are not a wedding. When I say I like a wedding, I do not mean that I like what interrupts a wedding, stifles a wedding, obscures all sight or sound of a wedding, or distracts everybody's mind from the very idea of a wedding. I mean I like the idea of a wedding. This will be quite enough of a paradox for my fiendish critics to digest. The actual words of the Anglican Marriage Service, for instance, seem to me to be a triumph of the English tongue at least as great as anything in Milton or Shakespeare; and it can be said of them more than of most poems and even great poems that to any one who can feel them they are always fresh and even surprising. And they deal with things that have nothing whatever to do with the paltry frivolities or passing fashions of our particular state of society; which (let us hope) is passing too. They are really worthy to have been spoken over Adam and Eve, in a voice that breathes o'er Eden, not merely in a breath, but a thunder-clap.

Next, we may consider the aspect of one recent

special occasion, in the sense in which it is quite truly called a historic occasion. The old forms of heraldry and chivalry, the ancient emblems of feudal or dynastic dedication, the varied colours of nationality, or the tremendous traditions of religion, which are by custom resurrected in such a ritual, are not merely false or merely futile things. They are generally a more genuine record of history than we find in the books of history; and certainly not so false, and not so futile, as the sort of journalistic history which is now popularized by the prigs who are the only educators of our uneducated plutocracy. They represent, of course, particular traditions and not the whole truth, particular loyalties and not all to which men should be loyal. But they represent them correctly and historically, and as they really were. They represent them much more truly than they are represented in the cheap educational works now so widely advertised, in which it is suggested that popular monarchies must have been unpopular because they had monarchs; or that ancient priesthoods must have been indefensible, because they defended themselves long enough to be called ancient. We hear a great deal in the historical world about the necessity of consulting contemporary documents. It is not sufficiently remembered that every costume or coat-of-arms, every flag or escutcheon, always is a contemporary document. Education itself might be educated, the happiest yet most helpless dream of our time, if people would only learn so much as the real history of a few uniforms or liveries.

Or again, the international aspect of such an occasion ought to interest any man who is, as every man obviously ought to be, both an internationalist and a nationalist. The fact that the bride represented the Royal House of Greece is alone enough to bring us back to a more liberal interest in Europe, which was one of the really marked superiorities of what is now derided as the liberal epoch. The queer provincial imperialism, now preached in so many parts of the Press, does not strike me as in any way superior to those hopes about the resurrection of Hellas, for which Byron died and Gladstone pleaded. Whatever agreements or disagreements there may be about details of diplomacy, every educated person must agree that the re-establishment of Greece was a landmark of history. It was the first modern constructive check, or obstacle, to the long unlimited and fatalistic landslide of Islam. Or again, the presence of the Greek priest and the grand Byzantine tradition of the Orthodox Church, side by side with the national tradition of Westminster, though neither is of my own cult, is a real reminder of the universal part played by religion in the past. It is certainly of far more interest to any thinking person than the unthinking ramblings about modern religion to be found in the modern newspapers. And the fact that the lady whom we all welcomed to the ruling family of our country is also connected with the heroic story of a Balkan people, may serve to remind us that epics and empire and a great peasant culture belonged to Serbia before politicians and pressmen had the fancy of calling it Yugoslavia.

Some of our journalists want to jockey us into a sort of Jingo pacifism; an insularity which essentially denies that we are a civilized country and a part of civilization. They would assure us feverishly that Dover can have no possible relation to Calais. They would insist that no single Englishman, in all history, has ever pronounced or mispronounced the name of Wipers. They must wonder artlessly why a seventeenth-century cannon in the Castle at Edinburgh still bears the name of Mons Meg. They may possibly be puzzled by the fact of an English country-house being called Blenheim or a London railway-station being called Waterloo. I do not know where they draw the line; but I must confess to a certain glee and gratification in the fact that this Royal Marriage did not even confine itself to a Channel-tunnel between Dover and Calais, but actually built a bridge that stretches across all Europe from the western extreme of Great Britain to the eastern extreme of Greece. It is the great defect of a mere mechanical machinery of majorities that it always leaves out that great democracy of the dead who are truly described as the great majority. Rituals and festivals, like those of a great national or international wedding-day, contain a thousand things to remind us that our countrymen inherit an experience much more lively and complex than any such local and temporary solution; and warn us against allowing the present to become more narrow than the past.